From the manger to the cross, Jesus announced the [...] sion of power—the last will be first, the first will be last; the mighty will be cast from their thrones, and the lowly will be lifted up. This book is about that Jesus—the holy troublemaker, the revolutionary Messiah. Craig dares you to join Jesus in the trenches and to reorient your life around the upside-down kingdom of God. What you have here is nothing short of an invitation to join the revolution of the subversive Savior who was born a refugee in the manger and executed as a rebel on the cross.

—SHANE CLAIBORNE, author, *Irresistible Revolution* and
Executing Grace

It's time to embrace a grown-up picture of Jesus. For many of us, the Sunday school picture of "passive Jesus" needs to be retired. So does the adolescent picture of my "private personal Jesus." It is time to meet "subversive Jesus," the Jesus who draws the ire of the elite by standing with and drawing attention to those who have been cast to the margins of empire. Craig introduces us to the Christ of the Scriptures, whose words and actions bring a corrective to the Darwinian society we have become. This book challenges us to love the prophets more than we love the profits and to hear with new ears how Jesus subverts the status quo of empire.

—SCOTT BESSENECKER, associate director of missions,
InterVarsity Christian Fellowship

After a lifetime of living among and working alongside some of the poorest people in the world, Craig knows a thing or two about the upside-down nature of the kingdom of God. Subversive Jesus comes riding a donkey, carrying a towel, welcoming children, feeding the hungry, and serving the least. And Craig knows him—really knows him.

—MICHAEL FROST, author, *Jesus the Fool*

This book is a wonderful example of the more honest reading and following of Jesus that is invading all of our churches today. It seems many have come to recognize that the "churchified" and pious Jesus many of us grew up with had little to do with the man and ministry revealed in the Gospels.

—FR. RICHARD ROHR, O.F.M., Center for Action and
Contemplation, Albuquerque, NM

Craig is a modern-day St. Francis of Assisi. Whether in one of North America's poorest zip codes or in the slums of Cambodia, Craig preaches the gospel through his life, not just his words. This is Craig's story, but as you read it, you may discover God's new call on your life. User warning: don't read this book unless you want to be challenged and your life changed. Do read it if you want to be inspired to walk in the footsteps of Jesus.

—KEN SHIGEMATSU, pastor, Tenth Church, Vancouver;
author, international bestseller *God in My Everything*

Craig is a prophet of hope calling for an urgent return to embody the subversive memory of Jesus. Craig writes with a keen eye for the substance behind our religious rhetoric, showing us the way to live and love in a world of wounds. When too many authors write about ideals that we all aim to embody, Craig flips that script and reflects on the gifts of what his embodied ideals have meant in his life, inviting us to join him in bearing witness to hope.

—CHRISTOPHER L. HEUERTZ, founding partner of
Gravity, a Center for Contemplative Activism;
author, *Unexpected Gifts: Discovering the Way of
Community*

You will find deep practical wisdom in these pages born of vast, hands-on experience that speaks to the breadth of human life—from what hospitality and child-raising looks like among the homeless to how to challenge injustice on cruise ships. This must-read refreshes and inspires, reintroducing Jesus as the life-giving, subversive, troublemaking friend of sinners that he was and still is. Read and you will want to join Jesus in experiencing "on earth as it is in heaven" here and now.

—BOB EKBLAD, founder/general director, Tierra Nueva
and The People's Seminary; author, *Reading the Bible
with the Damned* and *A New Christian Manifesto*

SUBVERSIVE

JESUS

SUBVERSIVE JESUS

AN ADVENTURE
IN JUSTICE, MERCY, & FAITHFULNESS
—— IN A BROKEN WORLD ——

CRAIG GREENFIELD

ZONDERVAN

Subversive Jesus
Copyright © 2016 by Craig Greenfield

Requests for information should be addressed to:
Zondervan, 3900 Sparks Dr. SE, Grand Rapids, Michigan 49546

ISBN 978-0-310-34621-1 (ebook)

Library of Congress Cataloging-in-Publication Data

Names: Greenfield, Craig, author.
Title: Subversive Jesus : an adventure in justice, mercy, and faithfulness in a broken
world / Craig Greenfield.
Description: Grand Rapids : Zondervan, 2016. | Includes bibliographical references.
Identifiers: LCCN 2015042431 | ISBN 9780310346234 (softcover)
Subjects: LCSH: Christian life.
Classification: LCC BV4501.3 .G7425 2016 | DDC 248.4--dc23 LC record available
at http://lccn.loc.gov/2015042431

Published in association with literary agent Jenni Burke of D.C. Jacobsen and
Associates, LLC, an Author Management Company, www.dcjacobsen.com.

Cover design: Tim Green, Faceout Studio
Cover photo: Nigel Swift/Millennium Images, UK
Interior design: Denise Froehlich

First printing February 2016 / Printed in the United States of America

*For Kristin Jack: my friend and mentor
in the subversive ways of Jesus.
And for my wife, Nay, who adds depth, wisdom,
and warmth to my life and so many others'.*

CONTENTS

PREFACE

A Note for You, the Reader

> Some people die at twenty-five and then
> they are buried at seventy-five.
> —ATTRIBUTED TO
> BENJAMIN FRANKLIN

I'm glad you picked up this book, because we live in a broken world, and people like you are needed. You are needed urgently. This book is your invitation into an adventure infinitely more daring, more profound, and more revolutionary than the life you thought you had to live.

You might think that you already know all about Jesus and the Gospels. That he is nice, tame, and predictable—the kind of guy you'd meet for coffee and a chat after a Sunday-morning church service. But I want to show you a side of Jesus that we have been too scared to embrace, the Jesus who sends tables and chairs crashing over because he is gripped by a passion to interrupt injustice. The Jesus who parties late at night with the wrong crowd because he is so radically welcoming of those at the bottom of the heap. The Jesus who turns water into wine because that's how he sees you and anyone on the edges—as water longing to become wine.

You might think that Jesus' most mind-blowing teachings should be systematically laid out in a theological textbook. With plenty of dull footnotes. But Jesus knows well that we are people of story and grit. We need to see theological ideas in messy human form so they can spark something real in our imagination. We need to see other people screw up so we can laugh or weep and imagine that we might dare to risk failure too.

Let me offer you the story of our experiment as a family. We set out to discover what would happen if we took Jesus' words seriously. When Jesus said to invite the poor to dinner, we invited our homeless panhandling friends, the local crackheads, and the prostituted woman from the street corner. They cheated us, disappointed us, and then became our best friends.

When he called us to bring good news to the poor and freedom to the captive, we organized Pirates of Justice flash mobs in downtown Vancouver. We wore silly hats and stripy pants, and waved a Jolly Roger flag for justice.

When he challenged us to love our enemies, we made homemade cookies and lemonade for the local drug dealers, and none of them showed up! This is the story of our pathetic attempts and regular failures to live out the most subversive of Jesus' teachings. Ultimately we were changed, and a grassroots movement arose for the poorest of the poor. We discovered Jesus, who wants to subvert and transform this world.

I'm convinced Jesus wants to take everything you think you know—about family and faith, service and suffering, justice and joy, and yes, even about Jesus himself—and turn it all upside down. The only question is, Are you willing to give him a chance? Are you willing to examine him in a new light? I've learned that where you stand determines what you see, so I'm going to invite you to stand with me for a while—in the slums and ghettos of the world, among the poorest of the poor. And see Jesus with fresh eyes.

Writer and activist Shane Claiborne once wrote, "Most good things have been said far too many times and just need to be lived."[1] So as you savor this story[2] and grapple with its implications, allow my journey to inspire your own journey. Allow Jesus to subvert what you think you already know. And you'll find that this book becomes an invitation to say yes to this subversive Jesus and do something courageous with your life.

CHAPTER 1

SUBVERSIVE
JESUS

> He has brought down rulers from their thrones . . . [and] has sent the rich away empty.
>
> —LUKE 1:52–53

I grew up in the church, and at a young age, I came to the conclusion that Jesus was "nice."

My grandmother had one of those old-school, nice Jesus paintings hanging on her wall in an ornate frame, in which Jesus is sitting on a boulder holding a perfectly white little lamb, his blond locks flowing around his serene face and manicured beard. This Jesus was nice, and I understood I should be nice too.

This niceness was much vaguer than kindness, for kindness is costly, truthful, and loving. Niceness, on the other hand—at least the way I understood it—was always appropriate, unfailingly polite, never disagreeable, and certainly not upsetting in any way.

As I grew older and began to look around the church, this niceness morphed into respectability, underpinning the way I understood that Christians should interact with wider society and the government. After all, Jesus was a good and respectable citizen who obeyed all the laws and never caused any trouble whatsoever. He never would have been involved with politics or protests or anything messy and controversial.

I learned in Sunday school that some of respectable Jesus' disciples, the Zealots, wanted a revolution, but they didn't understand that Jesus was just not interested in politics. He was interested only in saving people's souls so they could go to heaven. Inwardly, I mocked the stupid disciples for always getting the wrong end of the stick.

But as with all idols, cracks eventually appear, and my domesticated Jesus could not stand up to the rigors of life outside this respectable Christian bubble.

One day, bored with the predictable direction of my privileged life, I took a semester off from my university studies. I left my affluent, white neighborhood in New Zealand and boarded a long flight to Cambodia, where everything I had ever learned about Jesus was called into question.

Confronted by Injustice

The first time I walked into the Tuol Sleng Museum of Genocide in Phnom Penh, Cambodia, I was twenty-two years old and newly arrived in the country.

Outside the gate, I met a beggar with a bandaged stump for a leg and a rickety wooden crutch to provide balance. Most of his teeth were missing, and his grin reminded me of a friendly jack-o'-lantern.

When he saw me, he smiled more broadly, lopsided and cheeky. "Sir?" he said, thrusting an upturned baseball cap in my direction. A faded red, filthy T-shirt hung from his body. On the front of the T-shirt were four huge, peeling block letters: WWJD.

When I was growing up, those letters were etched into fluorescent-green rubber wristbands sold in Christian bookstores or printed on the covers of upbeat teen Bibles. WWJD might even have been a brand name, for all I knew. It was ubiquitous in the life of any nice church kid. But I had never seen those letters on the tattered T-shirt of a beggar.

WWJD: What Would Jesus Do?

I mumbled a greeting and stuffed a couple of bills into his cap, thinking, *It's the least Jesus would do.*

But those letters haunted me as I walked through that house of horror, stumbling from room to room in shock. Each space was a testament to the horrific violence that had torn apart the nation of Kampuchea. The Khmer Rouge had been careful to document and photograph each victim before death, so every wall was a graphic gallery of grief.

I paused to look into the eyes of men and women murdered by their neighbors, even their loved ones. And I asked myself, What would Jesus do?

Later that night, I tossed and turned in bed as I mulled over the question that had stolen my peace. How would the Jesus I know respond to a world torn apart by poverty and war and suffering?

Six months later, I returned home weary and broken. But my encounter with the beggar outside the genocide memorial had begun to reframe how I understood Jesus, and my prayers of struggle had sparked within me a lifelong quest not only to understand but to live out Jesus' words: the Lord "has anointed me to proclaim good news to the poor."[3]

I enrolled in my final semester at university with two certainties in mind. I would return to the Bible and seek to know more of Jesus and his love for the least. And I would one day return to live long-term in Cambodia in the slums. I wanted to know and love the poor so that they would no longer be the poor but my neighbors and friends.

I did not know that in setting out to change the world, I would end up being changed myself. But since my first encounter with the poor, I have found that if I pray for God to move a mountain, I must be prepared to wake up next to a shovel.

Encountering the Real Jesus

As I searched the Scriptures, it dawned on me that the Jesus I had embraced in my privileged upbringing might not represent such good news for the poor and oppressed. Respectable Jesus doesn't rock the boat. Tame Jesus doesn't upset the status quo or challenge the way society is organized. Domesticated Jesus doesn't disrupt injustice. I also realized that I wasn't the first to make this mistake.

In the nineteenth and twentieth centuries, the nation of Rwanda experienced an inspirational and sacrificial missionary effort from Western Christians of every type and denominational label.[4] These missionaries translated the Bible and built churches, schools, orphanages, and hospitals. They held revivals and prayer meetings, begging God to move mightily in the hearts of animistic people.

And the harvest came. Revivals swept through the nation—not once, not twice, but many times. Hundreds of thousands of people were saved and joined the church. This land, once known as a pagan country, began to embrace Christianity. Churches sprang up like mushrooms and thrived. The people, who embraced prayer and song, filled the churches, prayer meetings, and worship services. By the later part of the twentieth century, more than 85 percent of the population described themselves as Christian. By most measures, the nation had embraced the gospel. Followers were considered devout, fulfilling every requirement you could think of—prayer, Bible study, evangelism, church commitment—you name it.

On April 6, 1994, the Rwandan president's plane was shot down near Kigali Airport. This triggered the now-notorious Rwandan Genocide, which lasted approximately one hundred days. The Hutu majority swiftly and brutally slaughtered the Tutsi minority. Estimates of the death toll have varied between five hundred thousand and one million, or as much as 20 percent of the population.

In a Christianized nation, Christians killed Christians. In a country where only a tiny minority did not identify themselves as Christian, injustice and chaos reigned because ethnic designations—Hutu or Tutsi—were considered more important than a shared Christian identity. The events in Rwanda have shown us that professing Christianity is not always enough to overcome deep cultural, personal, or political values.

To be honest, I must admit that my own faith didn't significantly disrupt injustice in the society around me. Nor did I question the violence in my own heart, or my affluent lifestyle and ambitions. I had faith, by grace, in God. I had a relationship with Jesus, but for the most part it revolved around following moral rules: tithing with integrity, going to church on Sundays, not smoking, not swearing, and not sleeping around. By faith, I had received the gift of eternal life and would go to heaven—a wonderful place for me and anyone who believed like me.

As the cracks in my flimsy religion began to appear, I knew I had to get out of my privileged bubble and find a place where I could read the Scriptures from another perspective. I needed Jesus, the real Jesus. And I thought I might know where to find him: in a Cambodian slum.

The Quest Begins

I worried that my desire to live in a Cambodian slum—or in a cardboard box, as I liked to dramatically describe it—might not be such an attractive proposition for a potential spouse.

I had been invited to speak about my time in Cambodia at a little Baptist church. Only the most faithful, prayerful people will show up to church on a rainy weeknight to hear about missions, so the crowd was sparse but keen. I spoke first, then sat down. Next, a young Asian woman, petite but feisty, with her hair cut severely across the middle of her forehead, was invited to the front. Even on tiptoe she struggled to see over the top of the pulpit, and she shuffled her notes nervously. She began to speak of her remarkable escape from Cambodia's communist regime, the Khmer Rouge; her childhood as a refugee; and the welcome of a church community that had sponsored her family in New Zealand. With growing confidence, she shared her sense of calling to return to Cambodia, a calling she had cherished since childhood. As she spoke of her deep longing to return to the broken land of her birth and serve her own people, I knew that this cute woman would one day be my wife. I nudged my friend Phirun, who sat beside me in the pew. With a wink and a mischievous smile, I whispered, "That's my wife."

Afterward, as we all chatted and got to know one another, Phirun kept staring knowingly at her, his eyes twinkling with the secret. The woman told me afterward she thought Phirun was the one who was interested in her.

Her name was Nay, and she had fled Cambodia as a young refugee and eventually had come to live in New Zealand at the age of six. She grew up on the "wrong side of town," but through hard work and perseverance, she had gained an education and a career as a teacher. Now she was preparing to return to Cambodia, and so was I. The foundation of a beautiful relationship was already in place, and our friendship grew from there.

Nay's mother complained to her behind my back, saying, "Why do you go back to the place we tried so hard to escape? All this for nothing! Why do you go to university if you're not going to use your degree?"

But Nay had an unshakable sense of calling to return and serve her own people, and she was willing to hitch herself to me.

After we were married, we found one mission group called Servants to Asia's Urban Poor[5] that was training up Westerners to relocate into Asian slums, and we signed up to join them. They required a psychological test before we could be accepted finally, and we joked that it was designed to decide whether we were crazy enough to go. People thought we were noble, but a little bit weird.

I was reminded that Jesus' family had tried to restrain

him from going ahead with his plans because they were afraid that he had gone insane. Soon after that, the religious leaders accused him of being possessed. So much for respectable Jesus.

And so we moved to Phnom Penh and, for thirty dollars a month, rented a tiny shack that was built on top of another slum house and surrounded by neighbors in huts. Our claim to fame was the unused electricity pylon that rose up like the Eiffel Tower through the middle of our bathroom.

Our first home in a slum.

Relocating to a "Better Suburb"

Growing up, I often heard people talk about moving to a better suburb. Within the church, there would be seminars about "biblical finances," which were always presented by someone who was financially successful in the eyes of the world, someone who had moved to a better suburb, built a better house, and bought a better car.

But no one ever raised a hand in these seminars to ask whether an entire church seeking to move away from people in impoverished neighborhoods was consistent with Jesus' life and teachings. No one ever asked whether where and how we live might present good news (or bad news) to the poor. These were the questions we faced in Cambodia.

Good citizens (or Christians) weren't supposed to turn away from successful careers and affluence. Respectable Christians didn't throw in their lot with the poor. Perhaps the odd missionary, unfit for the rigors of Western life, or someone with great faith in God and a hugely sacrificial heart might lay it all down to pursue a special calling among the poor. But in the church, we called these people saints, and we put them on a pedestal.

Dorothy Day, who founded the Catholic Worker Movement and pioneered houses of hospitality for the unemployed and homeless all over America, refused to be called a saint. She didn't want to let Christians off the hook that easily, because she could not accept that some of us would follow a respectable Jesus who didn't rock the boat, while a special few would follow a subversive Jesus who turned everything upside down.

Yet when Jesus left the most exclusive gated community in the universe to live with the people he loved and gave his life for, he turned everything we know and believe about life on its head. That Jesus and respectable Jesus are bound to clash.

The Good News of the Kingdom

As Nay and I immersed ourselves in the Cambodian slums, I experienced Jesus' teachings in a different way. Certainly, the biblical world of filthy outdoor markets and beggars and dusty roads seemed much closer to the physical reality I was inhabiting. But now that I was surrounded by the world's poorest and most vulnerable people, Jesus' most provocative teachings came alive also. I realized that Jesus' teachings represented not just a ticket to heaven but also a subversive plan for heaven to come here on earth.

I couldn't believe that this Jesus had been living there in the gospel stories all the time, but I had been blind to him. As Pastor Brian Zahnd puts it, we Christians have demoted

Christ as the world's true King to merely "Secretary of Afterlife Affairs."[6]

This radical displacement from my comfort zone opened my eyes to the secret that had been hiding in plain sight: Jesus is not respectable or nice in the sense of being placid or uncontroversial. He is not necessarily a good citizen. Jesus is wildly and prophetically subversive, because beyond our affluent comfortable suburbs, not all is right. And something has to change.

The dictionary defines subversive as "seeking or intended to subvert an established system or institution." I was beginning to see that this is exactly what Jesus came to do. He did not come to overthrow a particular government or even win an election. Rather, he came to subvert and undermine the kingdom of this world, the status quo, by establishing a *new kingdom*, the kingdom of God. This was not just pie in the sky but a new and beautiful vision that would be worked out here on earth, as it is in heaven.

The words of Jesus—repent and believe in the gospel, the good news of the kingdom—pierced my heart as I began to understand what this upside-down kingdom[7] on earth might look like. For Jesus' life was bookended by an empire's standard response to anyone who is a threat: violence and brutal repression. From the time of the murder of every young boy after Jesus' birth to the day of his crucifixion, Jesus was opposed by an empire intent on maintaining the status quo. This kingdom labeled Jesus a troublemaker, rabble-rouser, dissident, community organizer, agitator, nonviolent revolutionary, renegade, rebel, and traitor. But none of this was a surprise to God, for God was preparing the world for the coming revolution.

Many of our Sunday schools continue to encourage followers of Jesus to embrace a respectable Jesus, an agreeable teacher with pleasant stories to tell about how to be good. But no one would crucify this Jesus. No one would be threatened by such bland personal morality. Instead, they'd invite this Jesus over for a cup of tea and a chat about the weather.

Good News for the Poor

Most churches don't spend much time on the disturbing words of pregnant Mary's song in Luke 1, known as the Magnificat. But during the British colonial rule of India, it was forbidden to sing the Magnificat in church. Gandhi, who did not consider himself a Christian (yet sought to follow the teachings of Jesus more radically than most Christians), requested that this song be read in all places where the British flag was being lowered on the final day of imperial rule in India. Free at last!

The junta in Argentina banned Mary's song after the Mothers of the Disappeared displayed its words on placards in the capital plaza. And during the 1980s, the governments of Guatemala and El Salvador found Mary's proclamation of God's love for the poor to be so dangerous and subversive that they banned any public recitation of the song. Though we have not yet officially banned it in our Western churches, we have done something much worse—we have inoculated ourselves against its message. Before he was killed by the Nazis, German theologian Dietrich Bonhoeffer proclaimed the song of Mary is "the oldest Advent hymn. It is at once the most passionate, the wildest, one might even say the most revolutionary Advent hymn ever sung. This is not the gentle, tender, dreamy Mary whom we sometimes see in paintings. . . . This song has none of the sweet, nostalgic, or even playful tones of some of our Christmas carols. It is instead a hard, strong, inexorable song about collapsing thrones and humbled lords of this world, about the power of God and the powerlessness of humankind. These are the tones of the women prophets of the Old Testament that now come to life in Mary's mouth."[8]

The Magnificat is a freedom song for the poor, with Mary as the lead singer. No wonder it has been part of the church's liturgy since the very first centuries. It has been recited or sung daily by ancient monks and hermits, but our modern church has lost sight of the subversive dynamite hidden within.

Mary's proclamation about the subversive nature of Jesus' kingdom is documented in Luke 1:46–56, the longest recorded set of words spoken by a woman in the New Testament. Her freedom song reaches its peak with this revolutionary couplet: "He has brought down rulers from their thrones but has lifted up the humble. He has filled the hungry with good things but has sent the rich away empty" (vv. 52–53).

This is the prophetic announcement of Jesus' life and ministry, straight from the lips of his mother.

Now, I'll admit, mothers can sometimes overstate the talents and wonders of their sons. But this is just the beginning of a very disturbing trend. From the moment he emerged from the desert, full of the Holy Spirit, Jesus was stirring up trouble. The very first sermon he gave enraged the crowd so much that they tried to throw him off a cliff.[9] Have you ever heard a sermon that resulted in people walking out of the church, let alone wanting to kill the preacher? Most sermons I hear in church, including my own, barely cause someone to shake their head in disagreement. They hardly warrant discussion over coffee after the service, let alone challenge our lifestyles deeply.

Archbishop Oscar Romero of El Salvador once asked, "A church that doesn't provoke any crises, a gospel that doesn't unsettle, a word of God that doesn't get under anyone's skin, a word of God that doesn't touch the real sin of the society in which it is being proclaimed—what gospel is that?"[10]

Jesus' words threatened the core values of his society, and the people erupted in rage.

Then there is the dramatic and powerful clearing of the temple,[11] an action that most of us struggle to reconcile with what we have been taught about nice, respectable Jesus. Turning over tables? Sending coins and merchandise flying? Making a whip? Using it! Interrupting the system of commerce? Not very tolerant or respectable, Jesus! Not very law-abiding! Bring back nice Jesus, we might think. I'm getting scared!

Yet Jesus was not some nice, polite do-gooder. He was not an American pastor who preached personal responsibility, good citizenship, respectability, and American values. He was the opposite. He was a controversial, radical troublemaker who challenged the status quo and the religious establishment, all the while embodying a wild and untamable love for the vulnerable and broken.

He came to inaugurate the kingdom of God on earth as it is in heaven. He came to subvert the world as we know it.

The Upside-Down Kingdom

In some ways, it was incredibly difficult to follow subversive Jesus in an Asian slum. The daily barrage of crises—flooding, fires, the massive Asian tsunami—wore us down and often knocked down our friends, who were already struggling to keep their heads above water. The stories of oppression, exploitation, injustice, and heartbreak left us emotionally raw. For six years, we immersed ourselves in the struggles of our neighbors, and this was both a deeply wounding and healing experience.

But as we were faced with the reality of the poor each day, it was easy to examine our decisions in light of the lives of our impoverished friends, who might even ask us about those decisions, causing some awkward conversations. We could gain perspective simply by looking out the window or stepping through the door, because our well-being became tied to their well-being.

As we made friends and cared for orphans, we began to see Jesus transforming lives in exciting new ways. From early on, Nay and I were convinced that local people would be at the center of what God might do in a country. We prayed that a local movement of Christians loving their poor neighbors might be raised up.

Then one day we stumbled on an obscure Cambodian proverb: "It takes a spider to repair its own web." Using this piece of cultural wisdom as our catchphrase, we began challenging young Cambodian Christians to take on one vulnerable child each, a sort of grassroots movement of Christian big brothers and sisters. We dubbed the movement Alongsiders.

We wanted the millions of vulnerable children in slums and rural villages to have someone to look up to who looked like them, someone who had faced the same hardships and could speak the same heart language. Someone they could count on to be there for them. An Alongsider.

The deepest need of each of those children was to be loved. As Mother Teresa said, "Loneliness and the feeling of being unwanted is truly the most terrible poverty." Yet this is the hardest need of all to meet, since love can't be bought or traded, pressured or forced. It can only be offered freely.

Tapping into the massive population of young people was like tapping into a rich oil vein. God released a geyser of spiritual riches. Incredibly, this movement took on a life of its own as God's Spirit began to flow through the Cambodian church. Hundreds of young people committed themselves to walking alongside those who walk alone. As this discipleship movement spread, we appointed local leaders and stepped back from the ministry, thinking our part was done.

By the time we were being evicted along with our neighbors from our second slum, which was being bulldozed to make way for a fancy buffet restaurant, we were sensing that God might be calling us to a new place.

Over time, we became increasingly uncomfortable when Western Christians idealized our lives and romanticized our poor neighbors, all the while demonizing the very poor living on their own doorsteps: the homeless, the unemployed, single mothers, those afflicted with addictions or struggling in prostitution in the inner city. So after six years in Cambodian slums, we sensed God calling us to relocate again.

One day, I opened the *Cambodia Daily*, a local source of news. On the inside middle page was a report about the most livable cities in the world. Tracing my finger down the list, I came to our own city, Phnom Penh, right near the bottom.

At the top of the list I noticed that proudly occupying the number one spot was Vancouver, Canada. Not far from my birthplace, it is an amazing city surrounded by spectacular snowcapped mountains and nestled in a sparkling coastline. The land flowing with maple syrup and Tim Hortons coffee. Vancouver, the most livable city in the world.

Within a year, I was to find out whether subversive Jesus and his upside-down kingdom would make sense not just in one of the poorest countries of the world but in one of the most affluent.

CHAPTER 2

SUBVERSIVE
WELCOME

> When you give a banquet, invite the poor,
> the crippled, the lame, the blind, and you
> will be blessed.
>
> —LUKE 14:13–14

After six years of living in a tiny Asian slum shack, our arrival in Vancouver was a rude shock for the whole family. Our children refused to wear clothes, preferring instead to run around naked like their friends in the slum. At night, they pushed the unfamiliar blankets and sheets to the floor, even though it was Canada's coldest winter in decades. We were all used to a sweaty, tropical climate, not slushy snow and freezing temperatures.

This beautiful city of high-rises and high finance was, on the one hand, a playground for the comfortably rich and famous—a kind of Hollywood of the north, with movies filmed daily on the streets. A TV show was shot at our kids' school, and celebrity sightings were not uncommon.

Spectacular ski slopes were less than an hour's drive away, and both residents and tourists flocked to the gorgeous beaches and parks sprinkled throughout the city.

Yet in the heart of the city, nestled between North America's second-largest Chinatown and the popular tourist destination of Gastown, we found the Downtown Eastside, a tiny inner-city neighborhood described by the UN as "a two-kilometre square stretch of decaying rooming houses, seedy strip bars and shady pawn shops." It was also home to five thousand crack cocaine, meth, and heroin addicts, hundreds of women trapped in prostitution, and thousands of homeless people.

Knowing we couldn't move into this slum by ourselves, we took several months to travel around to churches and share the vision. Eventually we managed to convince a handful of others to join us in forming a small Christian community. My mentor Charles—a theology professor and longtime missions advocate who had a white goatee and little Gandhi glasses that made him seem even wiser—advised us against moving directly into such an intense neighborhood. "Take another year to gradually work your way in. Take your time, Craig. Slowly but surely."

But when temporary housing gigs in other neighborhoods ran out one after another, we grew frustrated, and I became impatient. Nay, the kids (then two and three years old), and some of the others in our community moved into a Salvation Army halfway house several miles outside the inner city.

I schemed up a faster way to get to know the people of the Downtown Eastside neighborhood. My fellow community member, Jason—a thin and bespectacled aspiring theologian who was prone to bouts of allergic sneezing—always carried a well-read Bible and was terribly afraid of bees. He also had spent eight months in the library studying everything the Scriptures say about suffering, so, at least in theory, I thought he'd be up for my suggestion—as long as there were no bees involved. "Let's you and me go sleep on the streets of the Downtown Eastside for a while. We need to get a taste of what the poor in this affluent city face."

"Let me think about it," Jason hedged. Thoughtful decision-making was an infuriating strength that Jason brought to our community.

Later, as I discussed the plan with Nay, she expressed concern for our safety and worried that we would be breaking the law. But as usual, I was impatient. "It's not illegal to be homeless. Relax! It'll be fine. We'll be fine." I've since learned that most women don't appreciate being told to relax. Nay swallowed her irritation. "It's Jason's birthday next week. You'll be sleeping rough on his birthday."

"All right," I sighed, "let's meet in a cafe. Bring the kids and we'll have a little celebration. But other than that, Jason and I will be outside."

Foxes Have Dens

Jason nudged his glasses farther up his nose and sneezed. The cardboard between us and the concrete did not keep the cold from seeping into our aching bones.

The words of Jesus, "Foxes have dens and birds have nests, but the Son of Man has no place to lay his head,"[12] played ruefully in my mind as Jason and I tried to wrap the tiny, thin blankets from a local homeless shelter around our shivering bodies that first night outside.

This was not quite as exciting as I had envisaged. But Nay and the others had prayed and commissioned us to be there, to learn something of what it was like to be homeless in the Downtown Eastside. I'd look like a fool if we slunk back after just one night in the cold. Nay would probably tell me to relax! Then she'd turn me around and push me straight back out the door.

So we persevered. Long sleepless nights, shaking and coughing in the cold, were followed by tediously boring days, hanging out in run-down parks and homeless drop-in centers. We felt groggy and dazed as we shuffled from place to place, trying to pass the time and connect with other guys on the streets.

Each night, as Jason and I tried to sleep in the filthy alleys of the Downtown Eastside, I wondered why overfed and over-confident rats seemed to be the most common inhabitants of the various places Nay and I had chosen to live. In our Cambodian slum they had swarmed over the cesspit outside our window, feasting on the waste thrown through thatch windows. Here, the rats crawled through dumpsters and alleys, feasting on the abundant waste of a society of excess.

My friend Joyce Rees says that if you want to understand the good news that Jesus offers for the poor in a particular place, you first have to discover what the bad news looks like. Those few nights of sleeping on the streets of Vancouver's Downtown Eastside, alongside the motley throngs of other homeless men and women, provided a glimpse of the bad news our new friends dealt with, right in the middle of one of the most affluent places on earth.

Unlike Cambodia, where there are no soup kitchens, Vancouver's Downtown Eastside is saturated with places offering free food. If you're hungry, you can get a meal every half an hour from six a.m. until nine p.m. Yet as Jason and I lined up for our free meals, herded in and out of these anonymous soup kitchens, we realized that the men and women we were eating with were hungry for more than just a hot meal. Having been rejected by their families and pushed to the margins of society, they were desperately isolated and lonely. For those "lucky" enough to have a place to live, 82 percent of the neighborhood housing was limited to single room occupancies (SROs)—tiny, cockroach-infested apartments. It was little wonder that so many turned to drugs to dull the pain.

During the excess of time Jason and I had to sit and contemplate, we learned that if the bad news of the inner city was rejection, isolation, and loneliness, the good news might look something like radical hospitality. We realized that Jesus would welcome these folks inside—not just into a drop-in center or shelter but into a family.

In Cambodia, Nay and I had been moved by the desperate needs of orphaned and vulnerable children. We had seen that the children didn't need orphanages or institutions to warehouse them, but rather needed families who would welcome them. Knowing that Jesus would have walked alongside the helpless and welcomed them into his life, we started a discipleship movement to mentor the people of God to walk alongside those who were walking alone.

In Vancouver, the lonely orphans and vulnerable children had grown up to become homeless men with long beards and women with matted hair. But like the orphaned children in Cambodia, they had the same deep need to be loved, respected, and welcomed into a family. They still needed someone to walk alongside them in their pain.

Our heads were not clear. We were filthy and smelly and could barely think straight. But Jason and I were absolutely certain of one thing: Jesus would welcome the men and women we had been meeting, the most despised and least welcomed people in the city.

From place to place, even Christian to Christian, a radical welcome would look different. But amid the Downtown Eastside of Vancouver, we knew what Jesus would do, and we decided to do likewise.

Welcoming the Poor, Crippled, Lame, and Blind

In the gospel stories, Jesus does not seem interested in the staged hospitality of the Pharisees. Nor would he be impressed by Martha Stewart's brand of contemporary hospitality—special candles, fancy tablecloths, and scintillating conversation. Rather, he seems drawn to the messy hospitality of welcoming those who have been demonized and rejected by society.

In fact, in the Gospel of Luke, Jesus instructs his disciples to invite the poor and the disabled to their parties: "When you give a luncheon or dinner, do not invite your friends, your brothers or sisters, or your rich neighbors; if you do, they may invite you back and so you will be repaid. But when you give a banquet, *invite the poor, the crippled, the lame, the blind*, and you will be blessed. Although they cannot repay you, you will be repaid at the resurrection of the righteous."[13]

In our Cambodian slum, we had seen our neighbors, who were living on less than a dollar a day, share their meager food with widows and people dying of AIDS. We had seen young

Cambodian mentors give hard-earned money or a cherished notebook to their little brothers or sisters so that they would be able to study. Among these, the poorest of the poor, we had seen glimpses of Jesus, and we had been inspired to act.

As we wandered through the streets of Vancouver that winter, we knew that if we were going to take Jesus at his word, we needed to figure out how to sit around the dinner table with the homeless people around us. They were North America's poor and disabled.

I Was a Stranger and You Welcomed Me In

Finally, we managed to rent a three-bedroom home for our fledgling community of five adults and two children. We prayed for opportunities to extend hospitality to our home-less friends, who were often struggling with addictions and mental illness.

One night, I waltzed through our front door with my homeless friend Billy, who had unkempt hair and wore a huge, padded jacket. "Nay," I announced with importance, "I've invited Billy to sleep on our couch tonight." I beamed, excited to be living out the convictions I felt God was stirring within me.

Billy wore the world's largest pants, without a belt to hold them up, so he always had one hand on his waistband. He extended the other hand tentatively toward Nay.

"Oh hi, Billy." Nay smiled warmly as she shook his hand, but I could tell something was wrong. Throughout the evening, she was kind and welcoming as we shared a meal with Billy, along with Jason and Amy, our fellow community members.

But later, upstairs in our bedroom, Nay confronted me. "How could you invite a stranger to stay without asking me first? I feel anxious about having someone sleeping on our couch with our kids in a room by themselves, even if we are all upstairs and he is downstairs. Who is this Billy? Where did he come from?"

"Relax!" I said (unwisely). "He's actually a pastor's kid, but he struggles with mental health problems and drug addiction. He's been on the streets a long time. He needs help!"

Inside, I seethed with indignation. I felt that Nay was attacking the very basis of my faith in Jesus. How could our marriage continue if we couldn't agree to welcome the poor into our home? I considered quoting the verse, "I was a stranger and you did not invite me in."[14] But I thought better of it. *How can we go on,* I thought dramatically, *if Nay is not as radically committed to following Jesus as I am?*

Nay responded slowly, softly. "Look, I am committed to Jesus too, you know. I want to welcome the poor too. I actually know what it is like to be poor!" Nay had lost her father to the Khmer Rouge and had experienced the hospitality of a church family in New Zealand, so she knew firsthand what the radical welcome of Christ would mean to someone struggling with loneliness. Because she was culturally Cambodian, Nay also embraced community and hospitality more intuitively than I ever could, but her posture was more cautious than mine. "I need more time to get used to this," she continued. "I need some warning before you bring someone home, and I need to know that I can say no if I feel uncomfortable, or if I feel someone might be unsafe with the kids."

I breathed deeply. Of course. Of course! I was being an impatient, self-righteous jerk. Nay was right to be concerned about our children's safety, and I would do right to be think-ing of her, my first love and commitment.

I knew that loving my wife and children should not be considered a sacrifice requiring compromise, but the basic foundation of my calling was to love my neighbor. If I could not delight in loving and serving my family in unseen ways, then what right did I have to be performing more public acts of love and service for the poor? As Stanley Hauerwas writes, "Love does not create marriage; rather, marriage provides a good training ground to teach us what love involves."[15]

I was deeply convicted about how easy it would be for all these radical ideas of love to be nothing more than a clanging gong. Inviting homeless folks like Billy to sleep on our couch, giving away all our money and possessions, befriending drug addicts and prostitutes—if these acts didn't flow from a true love for others, as demonstrated by my willingness to love my own family first and foremost, then I was just a pharisa-ical poser. My public actions toward the poor had to match my private actions toward my family, or my love was not authentic.

"I'm sorry," I whispered to Nay. "We can work this out. I promise."

Nay and I embraced, and I resolved to be more understand-ing and loving toward my wife, a journey that still continues today. I also realized that I needed to negotiate a few ground rules with Nay before plunging into the practice of radical hospitality to the poor and marginalized.

And luckily, Billy didn't turn out to be a serial killer—just a slightly unstable hustler. But his stay sparked some good conversations about what radical hospitality should look like within our family and our community.

Longing to Be Welcomed by Name

Along with Jason and others in our community, I made a habit of hanging out at the local homeless shelter a few mornings a week to drink sugary-sweet coffee in paper cups, eat day-old donuts, and chat with the guys. Nay spent time with homeless women at the women-only drop-in. We figured that if we wanted to welcome the poor, we'd better get to know them first.

Gustavo Gutiérrez's provocative words rang in our ears: "You say you care about the poor. Then tell me, what are their names?"[16] Inviting people whose names and stories we knew into our home seemed more honest and safe than taking in complete strangers.

One morning, as I wandered home from the shelter, I saw a girl across the road who had been in our home a couple of times. Hunched over in the damp Vancouver cold, and dressed in a short skirt, high heels, and tons of makeup, she had clearly been out selling her body for cash and drugs all night. I shivered in the freezing air as I waved and called a greeting. "Hey, Felicity, how ya doin'?"

Felicity waved back and hobbled toward me on her high heels, rubbing her pale hands together for warmth. I figured she was going to ask me for some spare change or a smoke. Felicity looked at the ground, then blurted out, "Craig, it's my birthday in a couple of weeks." She paused, and I could see color rising in her washed-out face. "Do you think I could come and join your family for dinner that night?"

I knew that Felicity's request had nothing to do with food, but everything to do with a deep longing to belong, a hunger to be welcomed by name into a loving family. I looked at Felicity and smiled. "Of course! We'd love to celebrate your birthday with you."

As Felicity hurried away, I wondered what that simple welcome might mean to her as she returned to her work on the cold streets. Felicity needed someone to walk alongside her, just as much as an eight-year-old orphan girl in the slums of Asia does. But I wondered how much capacity she had to receive that love after years of rejection and abuse, because I knew that those who needed the most love often had the greatest difficulty receiving it.

Two weeks later, we prepared some small gifts for Felicity and made a birthday cake, and the kids hung a homemade Happy Birthday sign on the front door. When the agreed-upon time for dinner finally came, our table was full with feasting and friends, light and laughter—but no Felicity. Outside the weather was grey and miserable, and several times, Nay opened the front door to check the street.

By the end of the evening, she hadn't shown up. I hid my disappointment as we gathered for our usual time of reflection and prayer. As we interceded for Felicity, we prayed that one day, we would celebrate a breakthrough together—a milestone of one year clean from drugs, her daughter's birthday, or her own birthday as a beloved daughter of God.

Later, as I lay awake in my comfortable and warm bed, I wondered where Felicity had holed up that night, still aching for the love and welcome of a family. I wondered if she was shivering on a street corner, hoping for a customer so she could get a fix, or if she had numbed her loneliness with a drug-induced stupor. I realized that our battle was not against flesh and blood, but against the principalities and powers—addiction, affluence, rejection, injustice, apathy—that held this city and its inhabitants in chains. I knew that these powers not only held Felicity captive but also enslaved me, the church, and the whole of society. In order to understand what Jesus meant when he said he came to bring good news to the poor, liberty to the captive, and sight to the blind, I would need to face my own privilege and my own complicity in the powerful systems that marginalized the oppressed and kept them poor.

Living in the Shadow of the Empire

Almost the entire Bible is written by people living in the shadow of one empire or another.

The first readers of our Scriptures were slaves and fugitives, fishermen and fools. They were the oppressed of Egypt, the exiled in Babylon, and the peasants under Roman occupation.

And so, it made perfect sense for Jesus to come as one of those underdogs of the empire—a vulnerable child with nowhere to go, his parents shuffled about by the Roman demand for a census.

There are really only two goals in carrying out a major census, just two reasons to go to all that extra expense and bureaucratic hassle to count every head in the entire Roman world.[17] The first is to determine the number of people who can pay taxes, and the second is to figure out the number of men who can fight in an army. Money and power. The birth of Christ took place in the shadow of the twin pillars of empire: economic power and military might.

When Jesus' cousin John was asked what it means to

repent, he directly addressed the representatives of those two pillars of empire by calling on the tax collectors (representing economic power) and the soldiers (representing military might) to act justly and turn away from the ways of the empire.[18]

Then Jesus came preaching an alternative to empire. Something he called the kingdom of God (or, as Matthew calls it, the kingdom of heaven).

Jesus' subversive upside-down kingdom stands in stark contrast to empire. It's something that will come on earth as it is in heaven.

Where empire rides a white military horse and wields weapons of shock and awe, the upside-down kingdom rides a donkey's back and says, "Love your enemy, even if he crucifies you."

Where empire consolidates power and says, "My way or the highway," the upside-down kingdom kneels with a towel and washes feet, saying, "I come to serve."

Where empire honors the influential and celebrates the celebrity, the upside-down kingdom welcomes little children and gives food to the hungry.

Where empire is about power and status and tax breaks for the rich, the upside-down kingdom is about unemployed fishermen, rejected bureaucrats, a prostitute, and some failed revolutionaries.

Where empire is a rat race to the top, the upside-down kingdom says the last should be first, losers are winners, and the most important among us will do the dishes.

Such an alternative to the empire could lead to only one thing—the leader being silenced and murdered by the state![19]

Building a New Society in
the Shell of the Old

As we sought to live out Jesus' vision of an upside-down kingdom in the Downtown Eastside of Vancouver, we began to have an open table at six p.m., trusting God to provide enough food and welcoming whoever showed up for dinner and fellowship. Most nights, there were between five and twenty-five extra people on top of the dozen or so living in the house. Our motto, cheerfully borrowed from the Catholic Workers, was, "Cook too much food. Invite too many people."

As a community, we had agreed that anyone could veto the decision to allow someone to stay overnight if they felt unsafe. Because we were all inspired by the same vision, we spread the load and made sure there were enough people around to deal with security issues, as well as keep an eye on the kids.

We were inspired by St. Francis, who had an encounter with God that led him to strip off his rich clothes and walk away from a life of comfort in order to devote himself to solitude, prayer, and the service of the poor. Francis was deeply humiliated the first day he took a beggar's sack, walked with it into town, and went begging from door to door. He put all the collected food in a bowl, and sitting down to eat, felt sickened. What was this fetid gruel? Perhaps an old fish head, some turnips, and some fruit, well past any expiration date. Finally he overcame his disgust and consumed the foul mixture. And it truly seemed to him as if he had never tasted such a delicious meal. Francis thanked God, who had transformed the bitterness into sweetness for him and had increased his strength with the nourishment.

In the Downtown Eastside, supermarkets gave their expired food to local soup kitchens, and in turn those soup kitchens allowed us to collect their excess from the back door. Whatever was left would end up as swine food in this city of abundance. So, several times a week, we would carry our loot, overflowing boxes of pungent-but-edible treasure, back to our home to be shared that night with our homeless neighbors. Friends helped supplement these rich supplies with their own money or by dumpster-diving behind supermarkets. Most of our food had been rejected twice by the time we received it, yet it was transformed into the most magnificent feasts night after night.

Rent and other bills were paid from a common purse, each member contributing according to an agreed-upon monthly amount. And our own personal expenses were covered by other believers who were excited about what we were doing and wanted to free us up to do it full-time.

Like Francis, we initially balked at this level of dependence on others, until we realized that the poor cannot pay us for what we do. If we allow money to be the determinant of how we spend our lives, the agenda of those with resources to pay us will always take precedent over the needs of the poor. That's why lobbying for corporate interests is a multibillion-dollar industry in Washington, while funds to help solo mothers and the homeless are hard to come by.

We had learned interdependence with our neighbors in the slums of Cambodia, but within a fiercely independent Western culture, we were forced to delve deeper into the subversive practices of Jesus. Luke records that everyone had a different role within the body of believers, and in particular, Jesus allowed a group of wealthy women to pay the bills.[20] We adopted this model and were grateful to be part of the inter-dependent body of Christ.

Those who had been chewed up and spat out by the empire were attracted to our interdependent way of life, and folks started to come and go from our home throughout the day and sometimes into the night. Within a few months, our spare rooms, couches, and even our balcony became a tangled mess of sleeping bodies as people sought a safe space out of the weather.

Samuel, who lived under a bridge and was traumatized by past abuse in the residential care system, found a regular place around our table. "You live like my native people," he enthused. Greg, a quiet day laborer in his fifties who was living on the streets, offered us a few bucks a night to sleep in our spare bedroom and bought a tub of ice cream for the kids several times a week. A huge, shuffling Indian named Ricky played bluegrass guitar and told tall tales on our front steps. Such friends became part of our extended family and were grateful to find a refuge from the harsh Vancouver streets. But it was only a matter of time before the empire struck back.

CHAPTER 3

SUBVERSIVE

SHARING

> It's no use walking anywhere to preach
> unless our walking is our preaching.
>
> —ST. FRANCIS

A city inspector knocked at our door.

"We've received a complaint from the neighbors about drug activity on your premises," he said, shifting his briefcase from one hand to the other.

Knowing our place was drug-free, I welcomed him in, albeit somewhat nervously.

"This is the lounge and the dining room, where we welcome our friends for dinner," I said. I pointed to the wall, where the words, "In the Lord I'll be ever thankful. In the Lord I will rejoice. Look to God. Do not be afraid. Lift up your voices, the Lord is near," were beautifully painted. Our community member and resident artist, Ruth, had decorated our space with this prayer of thanksgiving.

I explained that we were not a soup kitchen but a mutual community of friends who shared life and meals together. I figured no government agency could stop friends eating together, no matter who those friends were or how outcast they might be.

It took more than an hour to show him the whole place, but by the end of the tour, he was beaming. "I can't believe what you guys are doing here," he gushed. "I'm going to tell my boss what a great job you all are doing and recommend no further action from the city."

"Thank you!" I extended my hand, relieved.

As I closed the door behind him, I sighed. *Yes. Thank you.*

Yet pushback not only came from the local authorities but also from the church. We had already been asked to leave an earlier rental home by Christian landlords who differed with us on what it meant to be good stewards of their house. They were upset that we were inviting homeless friends into the heritage home they had lovingly restored. We agreed to move on after just three months.

And our street friends also felt the stares when we brought them to church services. Offhand comments were taken as rejection, and I could see there was bridge-building to be done.

One day, our community was discussing how we could encourage others to engage our friends from the streets in a more mutual way, and someone piped up, "What if we did a progressive dinner?"

"You mean, go around and eat different parts of the meal at different homes?" I asked, vaguely remembering silly progressive dinners from my youth leader days.

"Yeah! We could bring our friends from the neighborhood to different church members' houses."

As the possibilities ran through my mind, I thought, *This might just be an upside-down kingdom kind of idea.*

A couple of weeks later, I announced what we were doing at a couple of local churches we attended, then waited for a response. But people were concerned. They wanted our guarantee that it would be safe, that nothing would get stolen, that no raping or pillaging would take place. Okay, they didn't verbalize that last one, but I could see the hesitation in their eyes.

Wanting to reduce the sense of risk, we explained to the potential hosts that we would split into different groups so there would be five of us at a time, and we would stay only an hour—long enough for a main meal or dessert and some "scintillating conversation."

And then, despite their misgivings, people signed up! To our surprise, we eventually had more than enough people who wanted to host our motley crew. So off we went by the carload, travelling around the city, singing with all the joy of a youth group on their way to some chocolate cake—though instead of high schoolers, our cars were full of people who had spent years in and out of prison and rehab.

Our friends from the streets just loved it. They were so touched to be welcomed into a normal home (other than ours) for the first time in many years.

But the deepest impact was in the lives of our affluent church friends.[21] That little taste of radical hospitality broke down stereotypes and barriers of fear and isolation. And it made them more fully human, more connected to their fellow human beings. The status quo was being subverted.

Subversive Charity

We see Jesus teaching a kind of subversive sharing in Luke chapter 9, when he is moved with compassion for the jostling mob of five thousand unfed peasants. His team suggests a common solution: Send them away to find their own food and lodging. In other words, let the people fend for themselves. Let them deal with their own problems. They should pull themselves up by their own bootstraps.

This is the way of the empire. Each man for himself. Survival of the fittest.

But Jesus doesn't buy their solution. Instead, he asks his disciples to engage the people and their needs. "You feed them," he says with a twinkle in his eye.

At this point, the disciples are incredulous. The needs are overwhelming and the resources so few: five thousand guys and their families, all with rumbling tummies.

Let's be real.

Who hasn't felt like this in the face of our broken world? We can't help feeling overwhelmed when we hear that one billion people live in slums worldwide, or that four hundred busloads of children die every day from preventable illnesses. It's hard enough to face the challenges of our own impoverished neighborhoods and inner cities.

Perhaps we don't open our doors to the poor because we are afraid that five thousand of them will show up and eat us out of house and home! We tell ourselves that their needs are insatiable and that if we give them an inch, they will take a mile. We worry that if we welcome the homeless into our homes, they will never leave and will take us for all we have. So we don't even go there, because we convince ourselves that we will regret it.

The disciples respond the way many of us do-gooders would. They wonder if they are supposed to go and buy enough food for all the hungry people. They imagine meeting the need themselves, with the pathetic resources they have on hand, in a one-way act of benevolence.

This is the charity model we have grown accustomed to: a simple transfer from the haves to the have-nots. It's the knee-jerk reaction of privileged people. And the disciples quickly realize the limitations of this approach to meet the vast need in front of them.

But Jesus shows them a different way—a way that is not based on individualism or charity, but subversive sharing. He wants to reframe the entire way relationships work in society. His upside-down kingdom is a place of mutuality.

So Jesus begins with the resources already available in the community. He takes a handful of loaves and fish from a little boy, thus including the poor and what they have to offer as a central part of the solution.

He prays, inviting God to work, to be central to the process, for it is only when we are open to the Spirit that we will be inspired to share and welcome.

Then he asks his disciples to organize the people, forming temporary mini-communities so they can break bread together, relationally.

And the rest is history. A beautiful miracle of sharing and abundance takes place that meets the immediate needs of the people and revolutionizes the way the disciples understand community transformation.

Do you have eyes to see what took place on that afternoon?

Jesus subverts the usual power structures. He undermines the status quo in a time when soup kitchens have replaced radical hospitality in our own homes. He neither leaves folks to fend for themselves individually nor allows his followers to engage in a one-way act of charity that would set them up as benefactors and beneficiaries. Instead, he asks them to share.

And he invites us to do the same, because who knows what might happen when we unclench our fists and open our hands? We might make some new friends. We might entertain angels unawares. We might witness a miracle. We might host Jesus himself.

When we encourage the poor to contribute what they have and allow the rich to contribute what they have, there will be enough—more than enough—for everybody. It is the miracle of miracles.

Later, as the earliest disciples of Jesus attempted to live out his teachings and the things that they had experienced together with him, they shared their bread prayerfully on a daily basis. Miracles reminiscent of the feeding of the five thousand broke out as people shared their property and possessions with all who had need. And the incredible outcome is recorded for us in Acts 4:33–34: "God's grace was so powerfully at work in them all that there were *no needy persons among them*" (emphasis added).

That's what transformation looks like. Subversive. Dismantling the kingdom of this world and building the kingdom of God *on earth* as it is in heaven.

Subversive hospitality is inconvenient, scary, and messy, so we Christians have cleverly tidied it away. We have outsourced hospitality to charities. Instead of welcoming the poor ourselves, we rely on soup kitchens and institutions. Instead of opening our churches and homes to the hungry, we are taught to "leave it to the professionals." This is the way of the empire.

We write a check to the Salvation Army and consider we have done our bit. We warehouse the poorest members of our society. And in doing so, we lose sight of how Jesus taught us to live.

Nay and I first learned these hard lessons from the poorest of the poor in Cambodia. In the Cambodian Alongsiders movement, we saw hundreds of young men and women with little more than a handful of fish and loaves to offer. In fact, they often did not have enough to feed themselves. Though they lived in tiny corrugated iron shacks or bamboo and thatch houses, these young people said, "I have something to share." In faith they reached out to walk alongside vulnerable children from their own community.

If you are willing to look carefully at the cracks, you will see signs of the upside-down kingdom breaking through the empire's concrete facade.

Subversive Inclusion

In our ramshackle little home in Vancouver's darkest corner, we tried to translate some of the lessons we had learned in the slums of Asia. We experimented with how to open our hands, hearts, and homes to those who were usually excluded.

For the next several years, we treated "the feeding of the five thousand" as a daily practice, just as the early disciples did. Our cramped dining room and lounge in Vancouver's inner city was pretty much full at around forty people, which was the maximum number God ever sent. Whether we fed twenty, thirty, or forty depended on the night. We began with what we had, and more important, celebrated what our impoverished neighbors had to offer. We saw in them the little boy who had faithfully offered his lunch. And we shared, rich and poor, together around the table.

Randy, who had tried to quit the bottle too many times to mention, brought us forty dollars out of his welfare check every month to buy eggs. "I'd just drink it anyway," he said gruffly as he stuffed the notes into my hands.

Jamie, a First Nations friend, cooked bannock (traditional fried bread) and other indigenous treats. Her friendship with Nay carried them both through many ups and downs.

Jimmy, heavily tattooed and toughened from years in prison, was always first to grab the dishcloth to wash dishes. Jesus had transformed him into a man with a gentle spirit and a servant's heart—a dear friend.

Lorna, who had been raped and forced into prostitution as a little girl on the streets of Vancouver, was trying to find a new pathway in life. She shared her delicious cooking with the crowds.

A cooking schedule ensured that no one was overloaded with work but that everyone could take responsibility. Before the meal we welcomed those who were new, saying, "If this is your first time, you are our guest. Make yourself at home. If you've been here before, you're part of the family. And you know that means doing dishes!" After the meal, the kids handed out Popsicle sticks to each guest, inscribed with different chores. Everyone pitched in.

Citing anthropologist Mary Douglas, sociologist Janet Poppendieck writes, "Charity 'wounds' because it excuses the recipient from obligations to repay that are deeply embedded in both culture and psyche and fundamental to human social life."[22] This observation reflects the fact that no one feels good about taking over and over again without offering something in return. Reciprocity is a fundamental organizing principle of society.

Traditional charity can foster a "taking mentality" that creates dependency and strips recipients of their dignity. Even worse, charity often violates the Golden Rule of community development: Never do for someone what they can do for themselves.

We knew that our friends from the streets had a lot to contribute. They just needed an opportunity.

But it wasn't long before we came face-to-face with the messiness of living on the edges of society with those who struggle—for we cannot separate the beauty and goodness of subversive hospitality from its challenges.

Subversive Boundaries

Benny was a broken and angry man who had been in and out of prison since age sixteen, when he had shot a cop in a robbery gone wrong. Before that, he had been shifted from one foster home to another. I don't know how old he was when he was first raped—perhaps eight or nine years old. As a result, Benny felt abuse and rejection in the most innocent interactions, and often lashed out to protect himself.

Along with everyone else that God sent into our lives, we welcomed Benny into our home and family and spent hours listening to him and playing guitar with him. But whenever Benny showed up, a fight could be an instant away.

"What are you looking at?" he would suddenly yell accusingly at another regular. And then two big men would be standing toe-to-toe, staring each other down.

Benny's abusive behavior created an unsafe atmosphere for others, especially the women in our community, whom Benny sometimes treated with contempt. Nay handled Benny with incredible strength and grace, but others felt intimidated.

Around this time, Nay introduced me to the popular book *Boundaries* by Drs. Cloud and Townsend. At first I scoffed. I had seen too many people use boundaries as an excuse to hold the poor at arm's length, to cop out of subversive hospitality. So I wanted nothing to do with the concept of boundaries, dismissing it as an easy exit for wimps and pew sitters. But as our community struggled to create a physically and psychologically safe atmosphere, Nay's wisdom about boundaries became a key part of our rhythm for a subversive life.

My friend Dave Andrews, who has established Christian communities in India and Australia, has developed a handy rule of thumb for Christian communities. He says, "Bizarre behavior is okay. Abusive behavior is not okay."

In the empire, it is the opposite. Being different or weird guarantees a person will be shunned, censored, or thrown in a psychiatric ward, whereas being abusive and disrespectful toward others is often considered tough and admirable.

But we didn't march to the beat of the empire, so we never batted an eye at the guy who came in wearing pink tights, makeup, and a tutu. We never worried about the insane ramblings of our friends who had bad mental health days. Instead we made it clear that respect for one another was nonnegotiable. No abuse or disrespect would be tolerated within the walls of our home.

Everyone on the streets and anyone who has been in prison understands and embraces the concept of respect.

Interestingly, the street definition of respect was a far cry from many churches' definition of respect. One upholds the dignity and value of all people no matter how messed up they are; the other wears a mask that says, "I am not messed up at all."

One day, when Benny came around in an angry mood and made some threats of physical violence, I sat down with him and said we loved him, but he was going to need to get some help with anger management before coming back inside our home. We would be glad to find him a course, pay any course fees, and even drive him there each time. But we needed to create a safe space by reestablishing mutual respect.

Of course, this felt like rejection for Benny. For folks who have experienced rejection all their lives, raw wounds are rent open again when they rub up against boundaries. So Benny stormed off, swearing and cursing.

Benny did come back, time and time again. Each time we met him at the door, holding back our sorrow, not allowing him into the house but offering to go get coffee together and have a chat. We pleaded with him to take up our offer of help with an anger management course. But he never did. Eventually, I received an email from a mutual friend telling me that Benny had died, alone in his room, from a drug overdose.

I felt like an awful failure, like I had failed to love Benny hard enough. Failed to persevere. Failed to be patient. Failed to help him find the kind of healing God had for him. Those of us who practice subversive hospitality will forever live in the tension between our finiteness, our human limitations, and grace. It will break our hearts when we have to say no or close our doors.

To be inclusive you must learn to be exclusive. In order to be truly inclusive and welcoming to those on the margins, there will be times when you must be exclusive—to shut the door and take care of yourself—so you have something to give next time. Or you may need to say no to one person so you can welcome others. To be inclusive, we must ask God for the wisdom to know when to be exclusive.

Offering hospitality in a world of sin and injustice will never be easy. We need a combination of grace and wisdom, spiritual and moral intuition, prayer and pragmatism.

Who knows if we did the right thing with Benny? We had hoped he would learn some strategies and boundaries for himself, which would make it more likely for him to find community and friendship beyond what we could offer.

Jesus himself needed to withdraw from the crowds at times for prayer and communion with the Father. He also knew that the time would come for him to step aside in order to give the Spirit room. I had to learn when to withdraw so the Spirit could do his work, and to be reminded that those of us who care for the poor are dispensable.

In that place of tension, we need both presence and absence. Presence expresses solidarity, compassion, engagement, care, and love; and absence provides an opening for the Spirit to come along and bring restoration, healing balm, and power beyond the person who was previously standing in the gap.

Edith Schaeffer of L'Abri, a community committed to welcoming young people searching for truth, said, "Because there are more people than we have time or strength to see personally and care for, it is imperative to remember that it is not sinful to be finite and limited."[23]

What a rich treasure this is. It's not a way to cop out of being present with people who struggle, but a deep affirmation of being present—then of withdrawing faithfully and getting out of the Spirit's way. This doesn't let me off the hook when I erect boundaries out of fear; but neither does it excuse my playing God and refusing to establish boundaries between the transformative presence of the Spirit and the desire to put myself forward as a messiah.

I had so much to learn.

Subversive Good News

We continued to struggle with opening spaces in our busy lives. When our homeless friends turned up on the doorstep at the last minute and someone with a crack addiction wanted to help us cook, we learned that real hospitality doesn't happen on a schedule. People who live outside don't keep track of time and days the same way we do.

Mike, "the Smokes Guy," would sit outside the Radio Station Cafe all day long, making wisecracks and holding court as he sold folks their cigarettes. One smoke for a quarter, five for a dollar, best deal on the block. Though if you walked a block, you'd get the same deal from the next guy. He was proud of the honorable way he sold smokes. Rather than worrying about the legality of selling smuggled tax-free cigarettes, he was concerned with justice and mercy. So he would always spot someone a smoke if they were "jonesing for a puff" and couldn't afford it.

Mike worked outside all day, and he slept outside all night. He had some sleeping spots that were a cut above the rest—gaps in walls or under hedges where he was unlikely to be bothered. He hated shelters, and he had fought for a new housing development in the neighborhood to contain low-income housing units. He proudly told me how he had squatted there for months with other protestors, one of the few victories he could recount from his long tragic life. Born in a trailer park to a family that was out of control, Mike's life quickly descended into the chaos of drinking, drugs, and abuse.

I don't know how Mike found our little home on East Hastings Street, but somehow he made it to our place several nights a week for dinner. He often brought friends with him, boasting that this would be the finest meal they ever tasted. "And the best thing is," he'd shout, even though they were standing only a foot or two away, "they treat you like a human being. You don't have to line up or take a number or anything like that. You just sit down around the table and say, 'Pass the butter, please.'"

He always said that last bit in imitation of a genteel voice—"Pass the butter, please, Jenkins my good fellow. Righty-ho, jolly good!"—as if the ability to sit at a dinner table and pass butter around was the height of luxury and service. And I guess it was, since he was used to shuffling into a huge hall with two hundred other strangers to have a ladle of stew slopped on his plate.

But even more than asking someone to pass the butter, Mike loved to cook. To hear him tell it, he was the most accomplished chef in the city and had cooked at a number of cafes I'd never heard of. But what he lacked in specifics, he more than made up for in confidence. He'd often sweep into the kitchen and take over—which, I admit, we encouraged.

Especially me, because I hate to cook and don't know a radish from a turnip.

Around five o'clock, Mike would swoosh in wearing his huge, puffy red coat—filthy from years of street living. His hands were stained dark and were never really clean despite the rough wash he gave them before cooking. And whenever he did cook, I offered up fervent prayers that God would keep us all from getting sick. Though Mike would never be clean by my standards, that standard was trumped by my desire to include Mike in our life and give him the dignity of being part of the meal preparation. Mike cooked loudly and confidently, carrying the bowls out to the table with a flourish.

Then our meal would begin. A community member would welcome all who had gathered and invite us to be grateful people by singing, "In the Lord I'll be ever thankful." This moment of melodic prayer has prompted more than a few tears of gratitude and blessing in the midst of our neighbors' chaotic lives. Mike always sang heartily and out of tune.

One day, Mike got to his feet during the meal and banged his fork roughly on the glass in front of him to get our attention.

"Uh, guys, I think we should pray for . . ." And he went on to talk about some ice hockey player whose wife had died. Canadians and their hockey! I could tell he was on the edge of tears, and I was touched by Mike's concern for someone else's suffering.

"Mike, why don't you pray?" I encouraged.

I wasn't sure if Mike would feel comfortable praying out loud, but he bowed his head and clasped his grubby hands together. And we did the same.

"God . . ." Mike paused, squinting with concentration as he searched for the right words. "God. Help. Please help. God. Amen."

It was like a groan from deep within, a groan that held all the turmoil and brokenness of his life, a groan that the Holy Spirit imbued with significance.

As the general hubbub picked up again, I knew that I had witnessed authentic communion with God from the lips of this homeless man—communion I might not witness during weeks of religious service. From the dirt-caked hands of a societal reject, I had been nourished by simple food and prayer, a blessing for my body and soul.

Just as Jesus took pains to point out to his disciples the widow who gave little yet gave all, Jesus pointed out Mike to me that day. Mike reminded me that those who are not highly valued by our society have a central place in the kingdom of God.

Mike disappeared soon after that, and I heard later from others on the streets that he had passed away suddenly from an infection. I stumbled home, gutted, and that night we raised a toast to our loudest friend. We sang the words we had sung together with Mike.

At some point during that meal, someone said, "Pass the butter."

And I smiled. "Certainly, my good fellow."

When we define hospitality as entertainment—a carefully planned event executed with precision and grace—we miss out on the subversive sharing that Jesus invited his followers to taste as they ate a meal with strangers. When we focus on fine foods and clever cocktails that will impress our family, friends, and those who can benefit us in some way, we miss out on the opportunity to build relationships of love and care with others. Jesus placed this kind of radical hospitality at the center of his new kingdom, a subversive posture of welcome for everyone, especially those who are normally excluded.

And that is truly good news for the poor.

CHAPTER 4

SUBVERSIVE
PARENTING

> Jesus called the children to him and said, "Let the little children come to me, and do not hinder them, for the kingdom of God belongs to such as these."
>
> —LUKE 18:16

Like most fathers, I love my children deeply, but at times I have been stretched to the breaking point. They teach me patience. They teach me perseverance. They teach me how to clean up bodily fluids from the bathroom floor at two in the morning.

But most important, they teach me about the Father's love.

Once, when our daughter Micah was about two years old, we visited friends who had a trampoline in their back yard. My son Jayden bounced Micah, working hard to perfect his technique so that when he landed, he would blast his sister ten feet into the air.

As her tiny body took on wings, she flew higher and higher until gravity took over. Grinning widely, arms flailing with joy, she came hurtling down—slightly off course—and crashed onto the frame and springs of the trampoline.

At the moment of impact, we were all reminded that Micah had a good set of lungs. As she let the world know that all was not well in this particular back yard, her shriek expressed what words could not: "Get your parental butts over here and *help me!*"

We bundled her up and rushed to the hospital, where the doctors gave us the verdict: bad parenting. Actually, that was the verdict we gave ourselves. The doctors diagnosed a broken leg, which had to be set and covered with a gorgeous pink cast. The color pink was a crucial aspect of the healing process.

As you might imagine, my daughter was not impressed with her full-leg cast, despite its pinkness, which was usually her main criterion for choosing any outfit. And her relentless wailing ensured that no one missed out on hearing about her suffering. The only thing that soothed her tears was a hug from Daddy. We drove her home and dedicated ourselves to helping our little girl adjust to life with a heavy plaster cast. The next six weeks were not easy for Micah, who was tearful and constantly in pain. Trapped in her gaudy pink encasement, she needed more hugs, more affection, more attention, and more love.

Meanwhile, my love for my son did not change, of course. But my daughter was in pain, and I recognized that she needed more from me in this time of suffering. No one questioned this emphasis. In fact, we enlisted Jayden to help as a caring older brother.

Shortly after this painful incident, my white-goateed mentor, Charles, cryptically said one day, "Doesn't a father's love for his suffering child capture something beautiful about the heart of God and his preference for the poor?"

It got me thinking. Growing up, I was taught that no one needs to be singled out because God loves *everyone*, rich and poor. This is true of God; and in the same way, I love my children equally. I would lay down my life for either of them.

But some of God's children suffer greater pain, poverty and oppression than others on this earth.

Through no fault of their own, by the simple fate of birth, some were born into broken families, dysfunctional communities, or war-torn nations. They struggle with abuse, addiction, mental illness, lack of opportunity, or awful living conditions. And sadly, our society typically expresses the least concern for these children of God.

As I reflected on my response to my daughter's suffering, I began to understand what Charles meant about our Father God's particular love for those for whom most of us do not have any concern. Theologians call it God's "preferential option for the poor"—a special interest, even bias, that God has for the people at the bottom of society's heap, those who need more attention from God *and* from us.

So God's preferential option for the poor provides the formula for a response when we become aware of poverty and suffering in the world. We know that God is particularly concerned for the poorest of the poor, those who receive the least care, love, and protection in our world. As his followers, we are called to reflect his priorities and to respond as if one of our own brothers or sisters were in pain—and we are called to teach those priorities to our children through word and action.

I thought of God's particular care for the vulnerable children we had worked with in Cambodia. I remembered Chenda, who had lost both her parents before the age of eight. She lived in a tiny rural home, where she and her elderly grandmother struggled to survive. And I thought of the people who were becoming our friends in Vancouver—the most needy, the most aggravating—and how the loving Father God was hearing and responding to their cries.

Jesus promises that even though the empire is a cold and lonely place for the vulnerable, his kingdom on earth will be especially good news for the poor.[24] As followers of Jesus, we need to figure out what that good news looks like as we respond to those who are suffering because of poverty and oppression, whether a beggar on the corner or an orphaned child in a slum halfway around the world.

Yet God's heart for the poor extends beyond physical expressions of care and concern. For God wants us not only to care for the well-being of his children but also to see that they are central to his redemptive purposes for the world.

Powerful Weakness

A few months after Micah's broken leg healed, a homeless woman gave Micah a pair of shoes that she had found in a dumpster. "Sank you!" Micah said, her face beaming with delight and joy. To Micah, they were new shoes, no different from an expensive pair purchased at a department store.

My children have lived all their lives in slums and inner cities. Occasionally, people pluck up the courage to verbalize their thoughts: "Is it a good idea to bring up your kids in some of the world's worst neighborhoods?" Some folks suggest that we are putting our ministry before the welfare of our children. They wonder if it is good for them to be raised around so many "crazy" people.

Nay and I have thought long and hard about this issue, examining our motives and grappling with Scripture. Of course, we love our kids and want the very best for them. But we want them to grow up in a family where Jesus and his subversive kingdom come first—before comfort, before affluence, and even, if necessary, before safety. We're not raising them to be quiet subjects of the empire.

One day, as I walked with my children down East Hastings Street, I was struck by how much it reminded me of an Asian slum—filthy, vibrant, and filled with people. Everywhere we turned, there was illicit activity. People were crouched in corners, soliciting passersby—"Crack, rock, up, down, T3s, and Oxy, whatever you need, whatever you want"—or hunched over in shop fronts and doorways, searching in vain for a healthy vein.

Micah, who by her own declaration was "a big girl now, Daddy!" rode in her stroller, a crown of purple cardboard stapled into a circle and thrust upon her knotty hair. Jayden carried a scepter—the fallen limb of a tree that still sprouted green—and grasped my pinky finger with his other hand. The children regaled me with tales of tomorrow's spelling test and their class photo shoot, oblivious to the fact that they were walking where police, upright citizens, and people with nice shoes feared to tread. To them, it was just our neighborhood—not a place where wild things lurked.

Micah and Jayden were the only kids on the streets that day, and on every block, a small miracle occurred. The call rang out, "Kids on the block!" A harried man turned his head. "Kids on the block!" A scarred woman straightened up. "Kids on the block!" As that familiar call echoed down the street, people stopped what they were doing—a crack pipe palmed and shoved behind a back, a bag of rock stuffed into a pocket.

When a small band of tussling guys noticed us, one shoved the other, swore, and shouted, "Yo, shut up, man. Can't you see there's *kids* on the block?" As we walked, a wave of calm and peace rolled over the street, and people stopped fighting, swearing, and pushing each other around.

In these moments, God used the vulnerable and weak, the children and the poor to shed the light of his upside-down kingdom into Downtown Eastside's streets. By their very presence, my children produced behavioral changes among this street community that no heavily armed police force could have provoked.

In the past, some missionaries have gone too far in exposing their families to danger and suffering, but Christians may be guilty of the other extreme. In making our children into idols, we've lost sight of the central place God has for our kids in his purposes. Nay and I have learned that as we trust God with our family, we will see him at work—not only in our neighborhoods but also in the lives of our children.

The Israelites faced this same question of allegiance when they used the safety of their children as an excuse not to obey God and enter the Promised Land.[25] God called them out on their wrong priorities, and because of their disobedience they had to spend forty years in the wrong place. (The desert may have been safer, and maybe it had better schools, but it was clearly the wrong place.) Those children finally entered the Promised Land, but without their parents.

Children as Ministers

Soon after we discovered the power of Kids on the Block, I met Leanne as she stood shivering outside our church. She was coming down hard from a crack cocaine addiction and needed a place to crash. The next morning, after she had woken from a deep sleep, the children climbed onto her lap and thrust a book into her pale face. "Can you read us a book, Leanne?"

I could almost see the healing taking place right before my eyes as Leanne was treated like a normal person for the first time in ages. My children treat everyone who comes into our home with the same childish impertinence and feistiness, whether our guests are dirty and homeless or cultured and well-off. This shouldn't be a great surprise, since God often used young people to accomplish his purposes throughout the biblical story.

God used a ruddy shepherd boy named David—the youngest of all his brothers—to defeat a giant and lead his people. God used a boy king named Josiah, who at age fifteen sought the God of David to launch a national revival. God led a young prophet named Jeremiah through danger, prison, suffering, and exile in the wilderness to bring messages to the people and to those in power. God used a poor, orphaned, foreign-born teenage girl named Esther to save the Jews.

Rather than coming as a member of the wealthy and powerful elite, God chose to announce his upside-down kingdom by being born as a vulnerable baby.

Jesus placed children at the center of his reign when he said we *must* become like little children in order to enter the kingdom of God.[26]

So why do we coddle and marginalize our children, assuming that God will wait to use them when they are adults? God wants to use them now. This is the subversive way of Jesus!

CHAPTER 5

SUBVERSIVE
FAMILY

> God chose the weak things of the world to shame the strong.
>
> —1 CORINTHIANS 1:27

We had been in Vancouver a couple of years when I took some time out to travel back to Cambodia.[27] Because empire values so easily creep in and distort my thinking, I wanted to keep perspective by revisiting old friends in a developing world slum for a few weeks each year.

I also wanted to reconnect with Tom, whom I first met when he was ten years old—the same age as my son was now. Tom's mother and father both died of an AIDS-related disease, and he had nursed them through their final months. Before his mother passed away, she was little more than a sack of skin stretched over jutting bones. While I knew him, Tom became an official government statistic—one of 144,000 children labeled "Orphaned by AIDS in Cambodia." There were fourteen million more orphans like him across the world.

Tom had always been poor. He'd always had to supplement his family's income by scouring the dusty streets for Coke bottles or rusty Tiger Beer cans to recycle for pennies. He had lost all mementos and photos of his parents in a slum fire, which were common in Phnom Penh, where evictions and yellow bulldozers were frequent threats to the neighborhoods inhabited by the poor. He had nothing by which to remember his parents, who had once laughed and bantered with their kids over bowls of rice. When there was extra food, they would point it out in the quirky way of Cambodians, with an outstretched chin and pursed lips—"Eat up!" After the latest fire, Tom had moved with his siblings to a slum in the southern part of Phnom Penh near my house.

One billion souls—or one out of every seven people on earth today—live in such a slum. And this community was just another vibrant under-city, like thousands more spread throughout Asia, Africa, and Latin America. Such cities are filled with the poorest, most desperate, and most resilient people on earth: orphaned children and widows, somehow rising above death and despair each day.

Several years before leaving Cambodia, Alongsiders had become a nationwide movement mobilizing young Cambodian Christians to walk alongside those who walk alone, mentoring and discipling hundreds of kids like Tom in slums and rural villages across the nation. These young Cambodian Christians, the Alongsiders, were between sixteen and thirty years old and were blessed with energy, enthusiasm, commitment, and spare time. They devoured the Bible in our studies, learned praise music on battered, out-of-tune guitars, and gathered at least once a week for youth group. They were usually trailed by a couple of younger siblings, a cousin or two, and at least a neighbor's kid. It wasn't uncommon to have little toddlers turning up at youth group wearing no pants and a ragged T-shirt.

We trained these eager and available youth to pray, then to choose one orphan or vulnerable child from their own community to come alongside. They committed over several years to be a Christian big brother or big sister to that one struggling child—to visit and encourage them regularly, to take them on outings (usually involving food, I noticed), to pray together, and to welcome them into the wider church community.

The young folks weren't phased or cynical about smaller children. They were excited to be given a mandate to minister in their own communities. They told me they were tired of being considered tomorrow's church. "Give us a chance to serve today," they demanded. And so together, we birthed a discipleship movement from among the poor to reach the poor.

When we were first beginning, I wanted to make sure that Tom would be one of the first to be matched up with an Alongsider from a local church. The Khmer word for Alongsider, *borng toa*, was deeply meaningful for Tom, a boy with few living relatives, as it meant a cross between an older sibling and a godparent. When I asked Tom if he was interested, his mouth stretched into a beaming smile. "Sh-sh-sure!"

The radical welcome of Christ, offered to an orphaned boy through the church's extended family, resonated deeply within Tom, and his faith sprouted out of the scorched earth of his spirit like a weed after a heavy rain. When he wasn't at school or collecting cans, he could usually be found in his room, poring over his worn-out Bible. Soon after that, through the relationships formed through Alongsiders, a church started a fledgling congregation in Tom's community. His newfound faith family began to take shape.

Tom's life was still hard, but by God's grace and through the body of Christ, he had found meaning and a reason to persevere. He told me shyly about a handful of modest hopes and dreams he nurtured in his heart. He wanted to save for a motorbike, one of those battered old Honda scooters that hundreds of guys rode all over town, annoying tourists as they touted aggressively for business as moto-taxi drivers.

He also hoped to become a computer teacher. I wasn't sure how he would do as a teacher with his stutter, but I gave him my old laptop, and Tom promptly proved me wrong by opening his room at night to local kids for English and computer lessons. The children would fill his room and overflow out the door, giggling and laughing, pushing and wrestling for a prime spot—dozens of them with no place to go and not much else to do.

Youth Bulge

Like millions of others throughout the developing world, Tom and his young neighbors are part of a demographic explosion—a population bulge of children and youth. A staggering 90 percent of the world's youth live in developing nations.[28] Meanwhile, millions of children are growing up without parents, without job prospects, and without the support networks they need to navigate their way safely into adulthood. Yet there is hope. We believe that some of the answers to the "youth bulge" crisis in the developing world lie within this generation. As some of the most vulnerable members of society, they have a unique opportunity to bring about transformation within their communities.

Throughout history, young people have been on the forefront of every significant social movement for change. Now, across the world, uprisings and revolutions are stirring in young populations from Africa, to Asia, to the Middle East. Young people are willing to give their lives for a vision. The only question is, are we giving them something that is worth laying down their lives for?

Expanding Our View of Family

Jesus offered just such a life-changing vision to a wealthy young Middle Eastern man when he earnestly came seeking religious advice. "Good teacher," he asked, "what must I do to inherit eternal life?"

Jesus "looked at him and loved him." He said, "One thing you lack. Go, sell everything you have and give to the poor, and you will have treasure in heaven. Then come, follow me."

It is striking in Mark's telling of this scene that Jesus looked at this young man and loved him. It was love, not judgment, that motivated this invitation. That detail is so beautiful and important that it challenges me every time I read it. By asking the young man to give up his grasp on his possessions and join his subversive community of sharing, Jesus invited the man to embody the kingdom of God on earth. Yet the young man rejects this vision of sharing, for "the man's face fell. He went away sad, because he had great wealth."[29]

In Acts 2, we see that in the years following Jesus' death, resurrection, and ascension, many did respond joyfully to this invitation and "sold property and possessions to give to anyone who had need" (v. 45). In a beautiful outworking of Jesus' vision, all the believers chose to meet together daily and hold their possessions in common.

Today, too many of our churches have concocted a dozen ingenious reasons why these stories no longer mean what they say. We dodge, twist, and overspiritualize what is plain to see—that there is a costly economic component to our discipleship. And that cost extends to our families.

As the disciples gasp and splutter over this teaching, asking each other incredulously, "Who then can be saved?" Jesus lays out a practical model of kingdom economics that reaches deeply into how we conceive of our family and possessions: "Truly I tell you, no one who has left home or brothers or sisters or mother or father or children or fields for me and the gospel will fail to receive a hundred times as much in this present age: homes, brothers, sisters, mothers, children, and fields—along with persecutions—and in the age to come eternal life."[30]

Houses, brothers, sisters, mothers, fathers, children, fields. Why does Jesus focus on our concept of family when describing the kingdom of God? This list makes perfect sense when we see that the word economics comes from the Greek word *oikos*, which literally means household or extended family. Our finances and our family are closely connected.

For those who are called to foreign lands, we will physically leave our homes and families for Jesus' sake. But there is a deeper meaning in this call to forsake all for Jesus, a meaning that challenges our idolization of the nuclear family.

In the kingdom of God that Jesus is describing, which will be good news for both the rich and the poor,[31] our families will be expanded a hundredfold. Yet to be part of that sharing economy, we have to leave behind our narrow focus on the nuclear family and widen our embrace to include others, especially the poor, the orphan, and the widow. So the solo mom in my community becomes another mother for whom I am called to care. The elderly recluse, another father. The orphan or struggling kid becomes another brother or sister or foster child in my extended family. Such communal caring erodes the harsh boundaries that our contemporary culture has erected in order to protect our traditional (and idolatrous) vision of family.

Jesus is saying, "For my sake, and the sake of the good news of the kingdom, give up your tight grasp on your family and possessions. I have so much more for you. A hundred times more." This call invites us to dismantle the fences we have erected around family, tribe, and nation so that God can expand our vision until we see everyone as part of the extended family of God.

An Extra Child

When I was growing up, my parents knew nothing intellectually of "kingdom theology" or "missional communities," but they lived out these principles just the same. Mom and Dad turned their double-car garage into a granny flat and housed refugee families. Christmas Day was never just for our family but always included an odd assortment of ex-prisoners, social misfits, and long-term foster kids who longed to be loved.

I remember Neil, this ginger-haired guy who lived for a while in our garage. He used to sit in our back yard with his legs covered by an old tartan blanket. He would just sit there and chain-smoke, staring into space sadly. My mom told me he lost his job as the Stop/Go sign holder at a construction site. Apparently he got too overwhelmed by having to decide whether the cars should stop or go. So now here he was, sitting and talking to me for hours. I have no idea what we talked about.

And it wasn't just adults. Most of the folks who came through our house were kids. Dedicated to providing foster care for disabled children, my parents made sure our family home was a revolving door for foster kids with special needs. We welcomed children with Down syndrome, like little Tommy. Everyone called him Tommy Turtle because he looked like a bespectacled turtle poking his inquisitive head out of his shell. He would come during the school holidays so his parents could have a break. Tommy especially loved to hide my dad's car keys and smirk wickedly to himself as we frantically looked for them. I loved Tommy like a brother.

With all the foster kids around, I came out of my own shell a little. As a young boy I used to spend most of my time with my head buried in books. But these children were from very different backgrounds and mostly from homes without books. They drew me outside into epic games and running battles. We used the fruit on the trees in the back yard as ammunition and staged heroic battles that sometimes ended in tears. I am deeply grateful for my childhood and the model of radical hospitality that my parents gave me.

Throughout history, there have been similar movements of radical inclusivity. On June 7, 1916, a young Indian man named Vinoba Bhave, a high-caste scholar with an interest in mathematics, met with Gandhi. As during Jesus' meeting with Zacchaeus, Gandhi challenged Bhave to dedicate his life to something more important than the accumulation of possessions and knowledge.

Over the years, as the bond between Bhave and Gandhi grew stronger, Bhave became one of Gandhi's most trusted leaders, and eventually his successor. On April 18, 1951, Bhave met with "untouchable" villagers in a small Indian town called Pochampally, where the people told him they needed eighty acres of land to make a living. Bhave challenged the village leaders to help, hardly daring to hope for a positive response. But to everybody's surprise, Ramachandra Reddy, a rich landowner, leaped up and said in a rather excited voice: "I will give you a hundred acres for these people!"

Through one man's faithfulness and another's generosity, the Bhoodan (Gift of the Land) movement was launched. From that day, Bhave began to walk barefoot from village to village across India with a simple request: "Consider the poor as one of your sons—and give them their inheritance." Those with three children were challenged to take responsibility for a fourth, and divide their possessions four ways. Those with five children would consider the poor as their sixth child, and so on.

In this way, over the next twenty years, a total of four million acres of land was given for the landless poor. As Indian people with wealth and resources opened their hearts to the kingdom idea that the poor are their sons and daughters, a movement was born, and the world caught a little glimpse of God's purposes for the things with which he has blessed us.

I knew that I wanted to be part of seeing such movements spread, leaving behind my own emaciated picture of family and inheritance and allowing God to bring many more children into my sphere of compassion. The Alongsiders movement was an exciting start, but I knew I could not teach what I did not know, and I could not lead where I would not go. I wanted to press even deeper into these kingdom truths in my own life as well.

A New Generation of Alongsiders

As soon as I arrived in Cambodia, I went to find Tom, who still lived in the same community down the same tiny slum alley. Now in his early twenties, Tom was an up-and-coming leader in the church, active there most days of the week, whenever he was not studying IT at a local university.

Tom welcomed me into a tiny one-room shack, just a stone's throw from where he had started out so many years before. Tom had made it a home—not exactly *Better Homes and Gardens* magazine material, but he had made a real effort. Some fading photos, including an old one of me and Nay, were tacked to a board on the wall. Beside the photos were Bible verses he had meticulously copied out and pinned up with pride. He had a desk and a few photocopied text-books, which he had lovingly covered with cloth to protect from dust. He even had a cell phone precariously plugged into a shoddy wall socket.

When I arrived, Tom was sitting cross-legged on the floor, sharing lunch with a little boy who was perhaps ten years old. The boy's can-collecting sack lay on the floor beside him, as grubby and frayed as its owner. Tom and his young friend seemed comfortable with each other, laughing and chatting over bowls of simple food. Tom used his chin and pursed lips to point, motioning for the boy to take an extra morsel of gristly meat.

Tom introduced me to his friend and told me that he had prayed for three months straight before choosing this boy as his little brother. "God showed me who to choose," he said. "He lives with his family across the lane. They are dirt-poor, and the whole family scavenges on the streets each day. They don't know where the father is."

The little boy looked up at me tentatively and smiled. I looked deep into his eyes and saw the simple joy of being wanted—not discarded or abandoned, but truly wanted. In the eyes of this ten-year-old boy, who was not unlike my own son, I saw the light of hope shining through.

"Tom," I said, smiling as I sat down to join them, "you make a wonderful Alongsider."

Tom grinned. He knew what a difference a big brother could make in a vulnerable child's life.

CHAPTER 6

SUBVERSIVE
VULNERABILITY

> If anyone forces you to go one mile, go
> with them two miles.
>
> —MATTHEW 5:41

Back in Vancouver, our community moved into apartments on the 400 block of East Hastings Street, right on the border between Chinatown and the Downtown Eastside. With our Asia connections, this suited us well.

Monday morning arrived, and it was time to walk my children to school. We traipsed down the stairs, and the kids pulled their winter boots on. Keeping our shoes off while inside the house was a habit we had picked up in Asia.

I tried to push open the heavy, steel-reinforced front door so we could move our jumble of winter coats and schoolbags out onto the sidewalk and off to school. But the door was meeting some resistance on the other side. I shoved harder, using my shoulder this time, and eventually from the other side of the door came a nauseous groan. Someone was leaning on the other side, blocking our exit. I poked my head through the gap and saw a bedraggled woman, sprawled in our front entrance. She bobbed her head drowsily, and then, with a massive effort, rose to her feet and stumbled away.

As we emerged onto the street, it was obvious from the Vietnamese dealers and drug users crouched in each doorway that our block was ground zero for Asian drug dealing.

As the kids and I walked to school, I greeted each person and pointed to the entrance of our home. "There's kids living here now. Make sure you don't go in our doorway, okay?" They grinned and nodded. One or two gave me a dirty thumbs-up. Kids on the Block.

Over the coming months, we got to know a few of the dealers, and mostly they weren't sinister, just messed up. Many were deep in their own addictions, willing to do anything to get another hit. Without exception, they were estranged from their families.

I noticed that they had devised an elaborate system to avoid getting caught by the police. Some of the dealers seemed to be holding the cash, while others held the drugs and still others were posted on lookout to "keep six" (keep watch for the police).

Jermaine was a young Cambodian dealer with an ornate Khmer script tattooed across his neck that said *Piasaa Khmer* (literally "Khmer language"). Apparently, he'd gone to a Cambodian tattooist who took him literally when he said, "Yo, tattoo some Khmer language on my neck."

One day, I came up behind Jermaine in the corner store while he was doing a deal with the store owner. A lot of the shopkeepers along East Hastings Street had side businesses buying and selling illicit goods. I greeted him in Khmer after recognizing the Khmer script. *"Soksabbay dey? Twer ay tngai nih?"* (What's up? What are you doing?)

Jermaine spun around. Obviously surprised to see a white guy speaking his language, he stared at me, shaken. Then he grinned. *"Oh, soksabbay. Ot meein twer ay porng."* (Oh, I'm okay. I'm not doing anything.)

But Jermaine and the other dealers were doing a lot. They were turning our block into a nightmare. Buyers were shooting up rigs full of heroin and lighting up crack pipes in doorways all along our block.

Despite my friendly requests, some days I came home and had to step over whoever was passed out on our front doorstep. Often, my kids would have to step over needles or other drug paraphernalia left at the front door. Someone once lost bowel control and left a stinking pile of feces for us to clean up with bleach and a bucket full of soapy water. I felt like a preschool teacher, with the street as my classroom.

I didn't want my children, or the other children on the block, to be stepping over needles, human feces, and the bodies of addicts when they came home from school.

On our block, we met plenty of zany characters that we greeted without batting an eye: drag queens on roller skates, a guy dressed like Robin Hood in green leather and tights, folks walking around with pigeons or rats perched on their shoulders, a guy with chains draped over his shoulders. But I didn't feel so welcoming toward the dealers doing business on our front steps.

One day my friend Jimmy, a former gang enforcer with swastikas tattooed prominently on his body and face, came into the house and told me that Crazy Kenny was sitting on our front steps doing business. Crazy Kenny was a notorious Vietnamese dealer.

"You want me to kick his ass?" Jimmy asked.

Jimmy had lived his whole life gaining respect through violence. In the brutal, racist gangs he had been part of and the prison system where he had spent much of his life, any sign of disrespect had to be met with immediate retaliation—otherwise you'd lose credibility, which could cost your life. During his gang days, he was known as Black-Eyed Jimmy.

Jimmy was wearing his favorite T-shirt, which said Jesus Didn't Tap in simple black lettering. He'd had it made to remind himself that Jesus didn't tap out of the wrestling ring when he was in the battle. Instead, Jesus never gave up and took on suffering and pain because of his love for us. Though Jimmy had a dark past, Jesus had given him some freedom from his addictions.

If anyone could deal with our dealer problem, it was Jimmy. He had become my best friend in the Downtown Eastside. Before prison, he had been an enforcer for a dangerous biker gang, teaching lessons to those who didn't pay their debts by spilling blood and breaking bones.

With a few strategic threats from Jimmy and a bit of rough-and-tumble, I figured we could get our block back. It could once again be a safe place for children and residents. So part of me was thinking, Yep, Jimmy. Teach him not to mess with us.

But then the inconvenient words of Jesus came flooding into my heart: He who lives by the sword will die by the sword.[32] Love your enemies and pray for those who persecute you.[33]

Resisting these words, I argued, *Can't we just teach these evil guys a lesson?*

Again, the words of Jesus echoed in my heart: *Like the tax collectors? Even they will enter the kingdom of God before you.*[34]

Amid my mental crusade for justice, I often slipped into an us-versus-them mentality, where I was on the side of the right and good, and anyone who opposed me was wrong and evil.

Russian writer Aleksandr Solzhenitsyn also grappled with this tendency, but he came to the conclusion that "the line separating good and evil passes not through states, nor between classes, nor between political parties either—but right through every human heart—and through all human hearts."[35]

No one, not even our worst enemy, is beyond redemption; and true transformation is complete only when the oppressors are transformed as well as the oppressed. That's why Jesus commanded us to love our enemies.

Monk, writer, and theologian Thomas Merton reminds us, "Do not be too quick to assume that your enemy is an enemy of God just because he is *your* enemy. Perhaps he is your enemy precisely because he can find nothing in you that gives glory to God."[36]

I knew our battle would be won only when the drug dealers were also transformed by the love of God. Retaliation, bitterness, hitting back, taking offense, violence—whether of the fist or of the mouth—would never lead to life, but rather the death of relationships, communities, and hope. Patterns of vengeance are strategies of the empire that Jesus came to subvert. For when we live by the sword, the hope of transformation dies by the sword.

As some jokester put it, "It is only when a mosquito lands on your testicles that you realize there is *always* a way to solve a problem without violence."

As far as I could understand the teachings and life of Jesus, I was pretty sure that we were being called to forgo violence in any context. Somewhat regretfully, I shook my head and told Jimmy that we weren't going to be "kicking ass" that day.

After resisting the impulse to respond to the drug dealers with violence, our next intuitive response was to retreat and escape from the conflict. Fight or flight. A lot of people had already moved away from the Downtown Eastside, and those who had never lived there avoided it altogether or made sure their car windows were rolled up before driving through.

Nay and I considered our choices carefully. Should we whisk our children away from the used needles, bodily fluids, and passed out addicts? Though part of us wanted to flee, we wondered about the little girl living next door who had become good friends with our daughter, Micah. The child didn't have a choice where she lived because it was the only place her single father could afford. We didn't want to give in to the drug dealers and abandon everyone on our block who had nowhere else to go.

Don't get me wrong. God built those fight-or-flight responses into our DNA for a good reason. If you find yourself in an abusive or deadly situation, you'd be wise to beat a hasty retreat. Get out, like young David fleeing King Saul's murderous intentions.

In Matthew's gospel, Jesus faced a major threat to his life: "From that time on Jesus began to explain to his disciples that he must go to Jerusalem and suffer many things at the hands of the elders, the chief priests and the teach. law, and that he must be killed and on the third day be raise. to life."[37]

Jesus knew he was going to suffer and die. He could have fought back, calling down ten thousand angels, or at least mobilizing an army of supporters. He had his own Black-Eyed Jimmys who could cut off an ear at the slightest whiff of conflict. On the other hand, he could have avoided Jerusalem altogether and fled to save his life.

His disciple, Peter, tried to decide whether they should flee from the empire or try to fight back. "Peter took him aside and began to rebuke him. 'Never, Lord!' he said. 'This shall never happen to you!' Jesus turned and said to Peter, 'Get behind me, Satan! You are a stumbling block to me; you do not have in mind the concerns of God, but merely human concerns.'"[38]

Turning to the rest of his disciples, Jesus painted a subversive picture of how to confront challenges and threats with vulnerability and humility—even to the point of death. "Then Jesus said to his disciples, 'Whoever wants to be my disciple must deny themselves and take up their cross and follow me. For whoever wants to save their life will lose it, but whoever loses their life for me will find it. What good will it be for someone to gain the whole world, yet forfeit their soul?'"[39]

In this narrative, Jesus offered his followers another possible response to violence, for he refused to use force to achieve his goals. He never retreated from suffering unless it was God's will. As followers of Jesus, we need wisdom to know how to subvert tense situations by responding with love and vulnerability. Jesus opposed evil without mirroring evil, modeling for us a transformative pathway of humility and love.

So Nay and I sensed that we shouldn't run away from Crazy Kenny and the rest of the dealers on our block. But we were feeling threatened by the increased drug activity around our house, and we knew we needed to do something to stop our block from being overrun by drugs.

We wanted to lay down our lives for the dealers and addicts prowling around our neighborhood, but we weren't sure what Jesus' upside-down kingdom would look like in Vancouver's Downtown Eastside. As a team, we began to talk about how we might be able to subvert the threat of violence with acts of love and creativity. Those informal conversations in our East Hastings lounge expanded to include other local Christian community groups over time: Salvation Army 614, Jacob's Well, Saint Chiara. Together, we began praying and exploring what Jesus would do if he were facing a similar situation.

Amid our conversations, someone suggested that we host a block party on Welfare Wednesday. It was the busiest drug dealing day of the month, when our neighbors throughout the Downtown Eastside received their monthly welfare checks. Dealers were out in force on Welfare Wednesdays, tempting people to part with their money.

"Let's use laughter and water pistols," someone said. "And face painting and sidewalk chalk," said another. "And cookies," someone piped up. "Gotta have cookies." Someone else said, "And a prayer corner. For anyone struggling with addiction that day."

The ideas came thick and fast, and the essence of the "holy mischief"[40] we planned that day resonated as an upside-down kingdom kind of idea. We all felt we were responding in a way that mirrored the transformative pathway of Jesus. We wouldn't be fighting or fleeing but rather opening our arms with humility and love.

On that midsummer Welfare Wednesday, we celebrated all day long with music, children's games, sidewalk chalk, card games, and a healing prayer corner with couches outside on the sidewalk. Ruth painted designs on children's faces. Ricky entertained the crowds with bluegrass music. Our neighbors filled dozens of tiny water balloons so we could all join a refreshing water fight. My friend Jonathan parked his big party bus out front and opened it up for watching movies and playing Xbox.

We invited Jermaine, Crazy Kenny, and the other drug dealers, tempting them with our own pharmaceutical concoctions: homemade chocolate chip cookies. But they were nowhere to be found. The whole block was drug-free all day. People who were trying to stay clean and sober—on the toughest day of the month to do so—were excited and grateful for a safe space to hang out.

That day marked a turning point for our block. Something in the spiritual atmosphere changed, and we won a skirmish in a much bigger battle. We continued to hold Welfare Wednesday block parties for months to come. We had not turned that corner through force or aggression, but rather through a Spirit of vulnerability, love, celebration, and joy. And as long as we lived on that block, the drug dealers didn't come back.

With one exception.

One day, Crazy Kenny came back and rang our doorbell.

Our front door was painted with a colorful mural of the tree of life. And I'll never forget the day I opened it, and there stood Crazy Kenny, looking a bit sheepish.

In his halting English, Kenny asked if we could help him quit crack cocaine. He had heard that we sometimes took in people who wanted to quit drugs and helped them detox and get into longer-term rehab programs.

We called it prehab. It was a major commitment for our community because we needed to be with the addicts 24/7, praying and accompanying them through the detox period.

I hesitated, not sure if he was serious, and not sure if I really wanted to help. Was I willing to extend a welcome to the man who had caused so much pain for so many people? Could I love my enemy in such a tangible way, enough to let him sleep on my couch?

I could see brokenness in Crazy Kenny's eyes, and I knew God was at work in him. So I smiled. "Come in. We can help you out."

Following Jesus along the Beatitude Road

Crazy Kenny lived with us for two weeks. The first few days of prehab were always the hardest, as the toxins made their way out of the body. Most of our detoxers slept for the first two or three days straight, rousing occasionally for a hearty meal before hitting the bed again for more sleep. One of us stayed with Kenny at all times, praying and making sure he didn't run away.

When Crazy Kenny finally emerged from hibernation, I helped him apply to a longer-term drug program where he would learn the tools he needed to stay sober. His written English was lacking, so I filled in the forms myself.

The days and weeks that the guys doing prehab spent immersed in the rhythms of our life and community always made a deep impact on them. They experienced discipleship, an alternative way of life. Kenny was no exception, and when the time came for him to move on, I hugged him with affection. An enemy transformed into a friend.

As I hung out with guys like Jimmy and Kenny on the streets of the Downtown Eastside, I began to discover that teaching men self-control as an alternative to coercive control of others was a central part of discipleship—my own and theirs. At the heart of every injustice—whether it involves drug dealers like Crazy Kenny taking advantage of addicts, the slum dwellers being evicted, or brothel owners trafficking girls—is someone using power to exploit, dominate, or control another.

We often fall into the trap of thinking that the solution to injustice is to gain power, hoping that once the roles of power have been reversed, the coercion will stop. But every bloody revolution in the history of the world shows that this does not work. David inevitably becomes Goliath. The oppressed persons who seize control simply become the oppressors.

The use of force or coercive power to achieve our goals, defend ourselves, or make progress is a temptation we all face, and I have come to see that Jesus grappled with this temptation all his life. When faced with oppression, Jesus tapped into the fruit of the Spirit and exerted self-control rather than using his power and privilege to control others.

I felt daunted and sometimes discouraged as I tried to figure out how to encourage my friends to embrace the way of Jesus by turning the other cheek and choosing nonviolence. So many of them, like Jimmy, had such violent pasts. But I was learning that there is much grace along the way, and it needn't be all or nothing—at least not at first.

At first, Jimmy was less inclined to take only an eye for an eye; he preferred to smash your entire face to a pulp if you looked at him wrong. God gave the Hebrew people the Old Testament commandment to take only one eye for an eye in order to rein in the bloodlust that erupted whenever his people sought revenge. Later, Jesus brought a new commandment in the same Spirit: "Turn the other cheek."

Clearly the commandments are not the same, but as theologian and activist Dave Andrews writes, "the intent behind both of these different commands was the same—and that was to limit the level of retaliation taken in a world caught up in relentless cycles of revenge."[41] If Jimmy could develop self-control and learn to take merely an eye for an eye, rather than someone's life for an insult, it would be a huge step in the right direction.

One day, Jimmy came to me, really worked up because someone had called him a "f%*'n goof." Now, in the Downtown Eastside, goof is the most offensive insult that anyone could ever use. When I first moved into the neighborhood, I thought goof sounded trivial, like dum-dum or silly-billy—a name little kids would call each other in the playground. But people in the Downtown Eastside have been killed over the word goof.

I bit my lip, worried about what he might have done to the poor fool who called him a goof. "You didn't . . . hurt him, did you?"

"Nah, you'll be real proud of me, Craig. I only punched the guy *once* in the face." He beamed proudly. "Just once, Craig! Normally I would beat him to a pulp!"

He had taken an eye for an eye—no more, no less. I patted him on the back. "Good one, Jimmy!" We celebrated each movement in the right direction, each decision to limit violence rather than unleash violence unlimited.

Yet sometimes Jimmy's strides toward self-control seemed ineffectual in contrast with the reigning culture of violence that is spiraling out of control in the world. Disproportionate military responses to acts of aggression represent the global version of inner-city warfare. Presidents and military strategists of warring nations seem to meet any sign of disrespect with immediate retaliation in order to protect their credibility. Even the self-discipline of taking an eye for an eye would be better than the heartbreaking cycle of shock and awe.

Over time, as Jimmy embraced limited violence, he gradually moved toward the nonviolent way that Jesus encouraged his followers to walk. Jimmy and I walked this journey together because I was deeply aware of the violence that still lurked in my own heart, ready to erupt at any moment. I had to face this violence every time I encountered the irritation of something as benign as a tangled string of Christmas lights. Not pretty, but pretty violent!

Together, Jimmy and I wrestled through situations where Jimmy felt someone was disrespecting or cheating him. I came to see why Jesus said, "Blessed are the peacemakers"[42]— for they shall defuse "situations."

Yet the subversive, nonviolent teachings of Jesus within his great Sermon on the Mount have been largely ignored, dismissed as impractical, or explained away by many Christians.

In the culture of first-century Palestine, Jesus and his people suffered under the oppression of the Roman Empire. The peasants that crowded around Jesus to hear him preach were ruled by cruel masters who garnered profit by exploiting and abusing the laborers who worked the land. This is an ancient story: those who grow the food are marginalized as the powerful stand on their shoulders to get more land, more power, more resources to control. In a sense, the powerful eat the peasants' bodies, since the peasants' sweat falls onto the ground as they work the land, getting into the food the powerful eat. Yet Jesus did not confront the power-grabbing culture by riding into Jerusalem on a military-style warhorse. He arrived on a humble donkey. He taught his followers not to seek revenge when they were wronged but instead to love their enemies.

In this day and age, we need to remember the divine name that the prophet Isaiah gave to the promised Messiah: the Prince of Peace. We need to acknowledge that we cannot sanitize or control war, and we will never be able to set moral rules that will justify military action. Once we enter the cycle of war-making, it will control us.

We like to think we are fighting for justice, but instead we are fighting for just us—our side, our people, our children—over and against the children and families of our enemies. Even then our intentions are deluded, since those who profit from war are elites who get richer while the poor are sent off to the front lines of battle.

War does not bring peace. It always ignites the desire for greater violence and revenge in the hearts of our enemies—and so begins the vicious, never-ending cycle of retaliatory violence.

Dwight Eisenhower, one of the most celebrated US military generals during World War II, later became president and is remembered for his hard line against communism (both domestically and internationally). He wrote toward the end of his life, "Every gun that is made, every warship launched, every rocket fired signifies, in the final sense, a theft from those who hunger and are not fed, those who are cold and are not clothed."[43]

In April 1967, Martin Luther King Jr. gave a speech in which he publicly spoke out against the Vietnam War, indeed all war and militarism, declaring that we could not confront the evils of poverty without confronting "the greatest purveyor of violence in the world today—my own government." King stated, "A nation that continues year after year to spend more money on military defense than on programs of social uplift is approaching spiritual death."[44] After this, King grew more determined to speak out against state-sanctioned violence, and perhaps it is no coincidence that he was assassinated a year to the day after this great antiwar speech. Radical challenges to the empire inevitably lead to the leader being silenced and murdered.

Theologians Stassen and Gushee collected evidence from early church documents to show that for the first three hundred years or so, the Sermon on the Mount was the single most quoted piece of Scripture evoked for teaching, discipline, or doctrine in the church.[45] The church fathers regarded it as the key to Christian discipleship.

But after the conversion of Emperor Constantine, Christianity was co-opted by the state. The revolutionary sermon began to lose its central place in the church's teaching because it threatened those in power and subverted the authority of the empire. Over time, Christ's radical "blessed be" verses were sidelined and spiritualized away. Instead of "blessed are the poor," the church teaching began to focus solely on "blessed are the poor in spirit."

But when we sideline the subversive teachings of Jesus, we lose any hope of seeing the kingdom transformation that Jesus inaugurated with his life, death, and resurrection. *Blessed are those who seek peace, for they shall be called children of God.*

Following Jesus along the Path of Love

One lazy Saturday morning, I stood in the kitchen drinking coffee with others in our community, feeling relaxed and peaceful, when the back door swung open and Tim sauntered in with a big grin on his face. A burly guy in his midtwenties, Tim was a friend of a friend and had come in from out of town to do some renovations on our basement. We were trying to create more space to house the folks who were coming off the streets to quit drugs.

As a new Christian, Tim was eager to help. "Guess what I did last night?" he blurted.

"What's up, Tim? What did you do last night?"

"I painted over that demonic pentagram next door."

My mouth dropped open, and I pushed past Tim to the back door, hoping he was joking. Sure enough, the ten-foot high pentagram, which had been painted on our neighbors' back fence years before we'd moved in, was gone. Ironically, Tim must have done the whitewashing under the cover of darkness.

I turned to Tim and said, "They designed that pentagram to commemorate their buddy who died in a motorcycle accident."

"But it's a symbol of evil," Tim spluttered. "It's demonic!"

Swearing, I covered my eyes with both hands and sighed heavily, hoping that somehow this was not really happening.

Then I grabbed a bottle of wine and headed next door to apologize for Tim's act of aggression. I had recently been over there to deal with their complaints about the people who were coming and going from our property.

"You'd better come back when my husband gets home," my neighbor told me when she swung open the door. "He's going to be angry!" Then she added quietly, "We're not Satanists, you know. But that painting had meaning for us."

Later that day, I went back to face the husband, who refused to accept the bottle of wine—my pathetic token of reconciliation. As I stood in the kitchen, he unleashed a torrent of curses.

"Look, what we did was wrong," I said. My palms were sweaty, and I wished I could retreat from this conflict. My stomach was churning with tension. "What can we do to make it up to you? We have an artist—she could paint you a new mural. Or we could pay for a dinner or a hotel for you guys to take some time out. Whatever we can do to show how sorry we are."

My neighbor paused. He looked at his wife, then spoke softly. "I want you to paint it back."

I gulped.

Now, I knew it was wrong for Tim to paint over someone else's spiritual symbol, no matter how offensive to our own beliefs. And I knew that if he had desecrated a mosque or synagogue, it would have been considered a hate crime. Moreover, he had trespassed on their property. But painting back the demonic symbol ourselves?

I tried to explain. "You know, we're Christians, and we believe that there is a spiritual realm, and there is power in images. For us, the pentagram represents evil, not good—and we want to be people committed to goodness. To paint the pentagram back would be a significant spiritual act for us. I think we need some time to figure this out. Would you be willing to give us time to pray about it?"

"Okay then," my neighbor nodded gruffly, hitching a thumb into his black jeans. "I'll give you till the end of the month."

Worried, I trudged back to our house.

Our community meeting the next day was lively as we sat around our living room, debating the pros and cons of painting back the pentagram.

"It's like painting a curse on our neighbors. It's not right!"

"No, it's turning the other cheek. Laying down our rights as an act of love. It's the right thing to do."

The arguments went back and forth, and I could definitely see both sides. "I think we need to spend a week fasting and praying for a way forward," I said. "Let's ask God."

So we read Scripture and prayed for wisdom, asking what Jesus would do—what radical, vulnerable love would look like in this situation. If we weren't going to fight and we weren't going to flee, we needed God to show us a third way.

I sought wise counsel from my pastor, from my mentor Charles, and from others who supported our community. Some suggested painting the pentagram back but adding little crosses or something hidden. But I felt that would be duplicitous.

When we gathered in the living room a week later, I said, "He that is in us is greater than he that is in the world. We do not need to be fearful of Satan or his symbols because we serve God, who is our strength, protector, and covering. And we've got to lay down our lives for our neighbors. Let's show them the radical love of Jesus, who chose to submit to an evil system in order to demonstrate that love. I think we should paint back the pentagram, but in a spirit of love and worship to the One True God."

Though some agreed reluctantly, a week of prayer and fasting had brought us all together on how to move forward.

I went back to the neighbors and explained our position. "Jesus said we should love our neighbors, and we want to do this as an act of love for you. We don't do it lightly. Unlike a lot of folks, we believe there is power in images, and that image is not what we would choose for you. But we'll paint it back."

A few days later, three of us took white paint and gathered in front of our neighbors' fence prayerfully. Ruth, our quiet and faithful artist, had found the correct symbol on the internet—a reversed pentagram with the head of the goat of black magic in the center, two horns at the top, ears to the right and left, the beard at the bottom. It was originally a sign of antagonism and fatality—a goat of lust attacking the heavens with its horns. Around the goat and five-pointed star were demonic symbols and shapes, each with its own meaning. Everything would be as close as possible to what was there before, at least in appearance.

But our hearts were full of worship. God had given us a way forward that would mean blessing, rather than cursing, our enemies. The symbols would remain exactly the same, as they had been originally drawn. But each would be given a new meaning in the way of Jesus, who redeems and transforms all things—even demonic symbols.

We started with the goat's head. Our paintbrushes dripped with paint as we traced the long lines across the fence, thanking God for Jesus, the scapegoat of the world, who laid down his life to overcome sin and death. Spontaneously, we began to sing songs of worship to Jesus, the divine scapegoat.

As we painted the five-pointed star, it became a symbol of the universe created by God. "Thank you, God, for your creation—the stars, the planets, the earth, and all that is in it. We declare that all of creation is yours!"

While painting back these symbols of evil, we realized that we were walking the extra mile, turning the other cheek, returning blessing for curses, and responding to evil with love.

And as we embraced this path of radical, subversive vulnerability, our hearts soared.

SUBVERSIVE
CHARITY

> "What on earth are you doing?" said I to
> the monkey when I saw him lift a fish out
> of the water and place it on the branch of a
> tree. "I am saving the fish from drowning,"
> replied the monkey.
> —ANTHONY DE MELLO, SJ,
> *THE SONG OF THE BIRD*

With Christmas approaching and the cold weather closing in, we knew that hordes of outsiders would soon be upon us. Our neighborhood's unique mix of notoriety and accessibility made it an attractive destination for groups of well-meaning Christians who were looking to do their annual missions outreach. The Downtown Eastside had become a circus of good intentions.

One Sunday afternoon, Jason returned from a worship service at an Indonesian church a few miles away. He had joined the church to build relationships and practice the language, because he hoped one day to move to Indonesia.

ιg down beside me on the couch, Jason said, "I've got some bad news." He adjusted his glasses. "When I was at church this morning, the pastor announced that *I* would be leading a group to give out scarves and socks in the Downtown Eastside this coming week. I didn't even have a chance to object!"

I groaned and squeezed my eyes shut.

Too many churches see mission as something done to strangers during an annual trip to a "foreign" place, rather than something to be lived every day as part of a lifelong, place-based vocation. Jason and I both agreed that Jesus was a friend, not an annual visitor, to the broken.

To make matters worse, Jason had signed up our whole community to help.

D-day arrived, and a cheerful group of well-meaning Indonesian Canadians gathered in our lounge. I welcomed them to the neighborhood and gently encouraged them to make generosity to the poor an everyday way of life.

"Today is just a taste," I said. "When you go home, ask God for eyes to see those who are poor and struggling in your own neighborhoods. Then welcome them into your lives."

As I trudged the streets that evening with our merry little group, I encouraged them to get to know people as individuals rather than beneficiaries. We had some good chats and invited a few folks back to our home for a meal.

From that day on, I wrestled more seriously with the challenge of closing the gap between charity and community.

The Problem of Isolation

One of the difficulties with a hit-and-run approach to charity is that there is little meaningful interaction between those who are distributing assistance and those who are receiving it. Because of this, the distributors are left to guess why the homeless are struggling or what they can do to bring about change. A brief chat will not do. Activists are not politicians campaigning for votes, sweeping into a neighborhood for photo opportunities as we pretend to listen to the "local people."

As people of privilege, we make choices every day about where we will live, where we will shop, how we will travel, and who we will spend time with. Often these choices isolate us from those on the margins of society. Our isolation from the poor shapes how we understand poverty, and it drives how we respond to it.

For example, if we assume that poverty is the result of poor choices, sin, and laziness, then we will judge the poor for their situation rather than showing them compassion as Jesus did.

When I first met Joseph, he had been homeless for a couple of weeks. He was around thirty and was waiting for some resources to come through so he could get an apartment and get off the streets. A graphic designer by trade, he had fallen on hard times. To get by, Joseph was sleeping in the shelters and eating at the various soup kitchens around the Downtown Eastside. Before each meal, he was required to listen to a sermon.

Can you imagine listening to a compulsory sermon three times a day, every day, for years on end? Some of us can barely get through a sermon once a week. When we first met Joseph, he was sympathetic toward Christianity, but after some time on the streets, he grabbed Jason one day and gritted his teeth in frustration. "If I have to listen to *one more sermon* about the ABCs of Christianity, I think I'm gonna go crazy!"

There's something deeply unethical about using people's poverty to force them to listen to our message. It is not the way of Christ, who comes gently to serve and offer freely and not to force his own agenda on people. Those who find themselves on the streets will be much more receptive if we invite them to eat first and then give them the freedom to ask questions and listen to our responses if they choose.

The longer we lived in the Downtown Eastside, the more we came to realize that many of our drug-addicted and homeless friends were already Christians. The neighborhood was filled with people of faith. Though some were living through seasons of defeat and hopelessness, the last thing they needed was more condemnation and blame.

When Jesus heals the man who has been blind from birth, his disciples want to know who has sinned—the blind man or his parents.[46] But Jesus isn't interested in their desire to condemn or pin blame on the poor. He tells them that they encounter the blind man for one reason only: to bring glory to God.

More and more, our team was learning that one-way acts of charity would never bring freedom to our friends. We needed not only to learn their names but also to discover more of God's purposes for their lives.

Charity: The Opium of the Privileged

Perhaps the greatest philanthropist in history was Andrew Carnegie, who gave away almost one hundred billion dollars (in today's economy). Ultimately, he endowed 2,811 libraries and bought 7,689 organs for churches in order "to lessen the pain of the sermons."

Yet Carnegie was known as a brutally exploitative employer who emphasized efficiency over safety in his steel mills. Hundreds of men met an early demise because of his drive to lower costs. When a steel furnace exploded, Carnegie was concerned about loss of production, not loss of life.

He backed up his push for profits by hiring thugs to violently crush any resistance to his demands for lower wages and longer hours. After brutal twelve-hour days, seven days a week for years on end, most of his men were unable to continue working beyond the age of forty and were simply discarded without receiving pensions or retirement benefits. Carnegie was supposedly a pacifist, but the lure of profits enticed him to accept orders for weapons, guns, and finally even rockets.

As Henry David Thoreau once said, "He who bestows the largest amount of time and money on the needy may be doing the most by his mode of life to produce the misery he strives in vain to relieve."[47]

Certainly, Andrew Carnegie is an extreme example of how injustice and charity can coexist within the same person. But to a certain extent, all of us are individually guilty of taking with one hand while giving charitably with the other.

Thus charity continues to exist—and even thrive—in the midst of great injustice.

Walking the streets that night with the group from Jason's church, we gave out socks and scarves to those who were living on the streets. Rather than addressing their core need for housing by opening up our spare bedrooms, we alleviated the surface symptoms of their poverty, and the group went away feeling better having done so.

But I was left with the haunting question, Is it possible

that this kind of charity actually *impedes* the realization of justice in our broken neighborhoods?

Sociologist Janet Poppendieck says that charity acts as a sort of "moral safety valve" in unjust societies by reducing "the discomfort evoked by visible destitution in our midst by creating the illusion of effective action and offering us myriad ways of participating in it."[48] That's an academic's way of saying that we often trick ourselves into feeling better when we cover up cancer with a bandaid.

By shuffling the hungry into soup kitchens, charity placates the downtrodden and assures that the rest of us won't need to be bothered by protests or unruly behavior. Meanwhile, temporary homeless shelters have become substitutes for a housing sector that includes affordable housing for the poor. Food banks and soup kitchens have become substitutes for affordable, nutritious food and livable wages. Tutoring has become a substitute for an education system meant to serve everyone. Free clinics and emergency rooms have become substitutes for affordable healthcare for the poor and unemployed.

Martin Luther King Jr. once said, "True compassion is more than flinging a coin to a beggar. It comes to see that an edifice which produces beggars needs restructuring."[49] Today, I might substitute the word empire for edifice. Clearly, an empire that produces beggars needs transforming.

The little group that walked around handing out socks and scarves was less organized (and institutionalized) than the local soup kitchen, which proudly proclaims that it has been "feeding the hungry and the hurting since 1942." Though their commitment is sincere, we have to doubt their ability to change a system that continues to produce generation after generation of hungry people.

For a clue as to why nothing changes, jump on your favorite charity's website and have a look at the people who hold the power. Most likely, you'll see a board of directors made up of good, kindhearted, dedicated people who have benefited from the status quo. Charities tend to appoint a disproportionate number of older white guys who will bring in big money, which typically means that they are privileged and affluent themselves—or, at least, they are good friends with lots of affluent people.[50]

To put it bluntly, these are the people who build and maintain the system. They are tied to the edifice because it pays their salary, dividends, or investment profits. Since they have benefited from the system as it is, it is harder for them to see the need for change. Their charitable motivations may be noble, but there is an obvious conflict of interest. Those who hold the *most* power and authority in society are the *least* likely to want to change the system that produces poverty. And yet, these are the ones we've empowered to control the work of the charities that are supposed to serve the poor.

This is a similar blindness to the Christian call during the eighteenth century, to be kind to one's slaves and treat them well. Slave owners had a huge incentive to maintain the system as it was, so any systemic tweaks were minor. Changes were made without sacrificing anything too costly. What we really needed were those who would challenge slavery fundamentally, challenge the empire itself.

So where are all the people who can bring change?

Throughout the Old Testament, prophets were sidetracked when they joined the king's payroll and feasted at his table. Similarly, our societies have always tried to co-opt those who are most likely to advocate for change. Today the charitable sector employs the most promising community leaders, who realign the sector's priorities and spend time maintaining those priorities. If we're all busy running around raising money for charity or maintaining charitable organizations, who will be left to agitate for real change?

Because most charitable work is donor driven, the entire system runs on money instead of relationships. Thus many donors demand tax receipts because they don't want to give if they can't receive some benefit. Yet Jesus warns us not to pursue rewards on earth if we want rewards in heaven![51] Sadly, the very act of registering with the government as a charitable organization that can give tax receipts hinders groups from engaging in significant political activity that might actually bring about change for the poor, because any protests against unjust government policies could lead to the loss of charitable status.[52]

The Justice Road

After giving out socks that night, Jason and I swore that we would never participate in bandaid outreach again. We were thoroughly disillusioned with charity since it merely tweaked a rotten system. And we were becoming more passionate about *justice* as a way of addressing the systemic causes of poverty, and also about *community* as an alternative way of life.

We were inspired by Moses, who didn't bother asking Pharaoh for more food and medicines for the slaves. Rather, he insisted on their complete freedom, saying, "Let my people go!"[53] Then he led his people out of their enslavement and into the Promised Land, where they formed an alternative society.

We were also inspired by Jesus, who said he came to bring good news for the poor and to establish the kingdom of God on earth. In the first chapter of Mark, Jesus began his ministry by going into Galilee and "proclaiming the *good news of God.*" Jesus said, "The time has come. *The kingdom of God* has come near. *Repent* and believe the *good news!*"[54]

Jesus highlighted the appropriate response to his coming kingdom: repentance. Jesus used the word *metanoeo*, which means to change one's mind. This is not about remorse or feeling bad but about waking up to a subversive new reality: the upside-down kingdom of God. Jesus called it the gospel, literally the good news.

So when people ask me whether I preach the gospel to the poor, I echo the words of St. Francis: "It is no use walking anywhere to preach, unless our walking is our preaching." In other words, unless I am living the upside-down kingdom of God, it is simply absurd to go around talking about it.

Once we begin to live out Jesus' upside-down kingdom, there are plenty of opportunities to explain this Good News verbally and to invite people to participate in the kingdom. This includes Christians who need to be converted to the gospel all over again.

So let us give up on cheap charity that is divorced from a life of justice and proclaim the truly Good News of the upside-down kingdom of Jesus to the poor.

Generosity

Though Jesus never rails against those with six-figure incomes, it seems obvious that he would be resolutely against a six-figure lifestyle in a world where children are starving.

As we continued to build relationships with folks who were economically poor, I became more aware of the economic disparity that separated us. My sometimes frenetic consumerism seemed crass, and the words of Jesus spoke more deeply to me: *If you cling to your lifestyle, you will lose it.*[55] I realized that whenever rich people like me want to follow Jesus, we are invited to sell our possessions and give to the poor.[56]

And sometimes, as we see with Zacchaeus—a stumpy con man who was wheedling his way through life when he first met Jesus—this invitation results in a life-changing conversion and transformation. Convicted by the realization of what he has done to others, Zacchaeus cries out, "Look, Lord! Here and now I give half of my possessions to the poor, and if I have cheated anybody out of anything, I will pay back four times the amount."[57] Amazingly, as soon as he hears Zacchaeus's economic repentance, Jesus proclaims, "Today salvation has come to this house!"[58] Yet in our churches, this economic element to repentance and discipleship is often overlooked.[59]

Remember, Zacchaeus was only one of many tax collectors in town during Jesus' day, and he was only one cog in the wheel of the Roman Empire, which secured land and other resources for the rich by oppressing the poor. Throughout history, the vast majority of the individuals and nations who have lived comfortably by exploiting others have never come face-to-face with Jesus and his upside-down kingdom. They have never been invited to repent for their sins of injustice in the way Zacchaeus was. And so they have never heard Jesus say, as he says to Zacchaeus after his conversion toward the poor, "Today salvation has come to this house . . . For the Son of Man came to seek and to save the lost."[60]

Like the unnamed rich man in the Lazarus parable—the one who held on to "good things" during his lifetime and refused to share out of his abundance with the suffering Lazarus—these wealthy individuals and nations were never liberated from the bondage of their ill-gotten affluence.[61] When the rich man begs Father Abraham to "send Lazarus" to return and warn his family about the torment that awaits them, the haunting reply is: "If they do not listen to Moses and the Prophets, they will not be convinced even if someone rises from the dead."[62]

And because the wealth of the rich was never redistributed to the poor and oppressed, it was kept within the family, passed from one generation to the next.

And here's the kicker—I inherited my wealth. And you probably did too.

Somewhere along the line, some of my great-great-great-great grandfathers got rich off the backs of those they exploited. And some of my relatives enslaved Africans and sent them to work in the fields for their profit. And some of my ancestors travelled the world, plundering resources from Asia and Africa for their own gain. And some in my family were colonizers, who stole land from indigenous people and placated them with trinkets and liquor.

Though our ties to ancestral connections may be remote, the wealth and privilege we have inherited remains in our hands and in our bank accounts. That wealth, both my family's wealth and the wealth of my nation, is the foundation of my privilege, the head start I got in life. Though I didn't steal it myself, I have some responsibility for it now. Like Zacchaeus, I come face-to-face with Jesus and am confronted by the realization of what my privilege has cost others.

Jesus is standing beneath the tree we have climbed in order to avoid engaging the poor, the oppressed, the broken, and the marginalized. He is looking up at us and asking us to come down, so that we might encounter his upside-down kingdom and repent for our sins of injustice. He is waiting for the invitation to dine at our table, so that he can bless us with the hope of salvation for all.

And on the far side of history, as we continue along the journey from charity toward justice, we are invited to say with Zacchaeus, "Look, Lord! Here and now I give half of my possessions to the poor, and if I have cheated anybody out of anything, I will pay back four times the amount."[63]

CHAPTER 8

SUBVERSIVE

COMMUNITY

> Whoever believes in me will do the works
> I have been doing, and they will do even
> greater things than these.
>
> —JOHN 14:12

Charles stroked his white goatee and looked at me with his kind, wise eyes. "Remember, Craig, four friends brought one paralytic to Jesus. Not the other way around. One of the most important things you can offer others is Christian community."

Nay and I had now been living in the Downtown Eastside for four years. Charles had moved away from Canada, but somehow managed to visit Vancouver about once a year— usually just when I needed input or encouragement.

His words resonated within me, because the little Christian community God had birthed in the Downtown Eastside of Vancouver was a powerful and transformative gift that we were offering to those experiencing loneliness and isolation. Moving beyond charity, we were surrounding hurting people who were paralyzed by addictions and accompanying them along the road of healing in Christ.

In Cambodia, as Christian young people walked alongside their little brothers or little sisters, they were welcoming vulnerable children out of isolation and into the family of God. For children who were at risk and marginalized by society, connecting to a support network such as the local church was powerfully healing and transformative.

One by one, broken lives were being restored. Guys like Crazy Kenny were finding freedom. After Kenny detoxed from crack cocaine and got into rehab, I didn't hear anything about him for at least a year. Then one day, his Vietnamese friend Pete came by to visit. Pete had been in and out of rehab himself a few times, trying to get the monkey off his back, but he hadn't been able to make it stick.

"Out of everyone on the street, no one thought Crazy Kenny would get free of his addiction," Pete marveled. "He was the last person we ever expected to get clean. He's even gotten married!"

Kenny's transformation was encouraging, and he wasn't the only one. In our home, we had now accompanied well over a hundred men and women through detox and into local rehab programs. Not all were fully drug free, but a significant number had experienced the freedom from addiction that Jesus offers—and many had become followers of Jesus.

I knew that this fruit was a result of working together as a community, and I prayerfully gave thanks to God for Jason and Laura, Ruth, Tom and Ashleen and their three beautiful daughters, and everyone else who had thrown their lot in with us over the years to serve God by serving the poor.

Learning from the Margins

After our experience with the socks and scarves, I became more cautious about the requests our community received from groups who wanted to "come and serve" our ministry or people who wanted to "bless others" in our neighborhood.

So we started asking people to come as learners. We didn't want them to wear matching T-shirts that would clearly delineate who was serving and who was being served. We didn't want them to drive around in vans with church logos, or to carry cameras to capture their saintliness. We wanted them to come and sit and learn from the unlikely saints of the streets. For what the eye does not see, the heart cannot grieve.

If I thought a group would be open to learning from local people, I would say, "Yes, and I know just the person to show you around the neighborhood—my friend Ricky!"

Everything about Ricky was big—big and slow. He even played his bluegrass guitar slow, like thick syrup dripping down the side of a jar. Ricky was everybody's friend. You just couldn't walk fast with him, for he moved slower than a shadow in summertime.

Lilla Watson, an aboriginal activist in Australia, confronted the hordes of do-gooders who came to serve and help her people by saying, "If you have come to help me, you are wasting your time. But if you have come because your liberation is bound up with mine, then let us walk together."

These words could just as well have been Ricky's. When groups would arrive, we'd introduce them to Ricky. As tour guide, he would invite them to walk a few miles in his shoes (smelly feet and all), and they'd head off at the pace of a lazy snail. They'd edge their way through the Downtown Eastside and learn the important places for free food and fellowship, and where to find a sleeping mat that wasn't too full of bedbugs.

Then these groups would come back to our house a little wiser—and a little slower. Perhaps they discovered that their salvation was somehow bound up with Ricky's.[64]

Jesus calls us to leave our comfortable isolation and meet folks like Ricky. At the edges of society, we can be converted to a new perspective rather than remain blithely oblivious to their needs.

Though our initial engagement with the poor might begin with a short-term mission trip, it must not end there, because Jesus himself was known as a friend of the broken— not just a visitor. Our lives must develop an ongoing rhythm of interacting with and embracing those who are struggling.

Obviously, not all Christians can relocate to a poor inner city or slum, because affordable housing in these areas is already scarce. However, since over a billion people in the world live in slums, it might not be such a bad idea for more of us to consider it—at least for a season. It would certainly change our perspective about the challenges faced by those who are living in the slums.[65]

But we all can find and nurture crossover spaces where our lives and the lives of those on the margins have the opportunity to overlap. We might commit to taking public transit, or to shopping in more marginalized areas, or to frequenting coffee shops where the homeless congregate, or to worshipping at a church in an urban slum. In these places, we can engage regularly with those who are struggling. We can meet and learn from people like Ricky. And we can ask God to give us eyes to see those who are struggling in our midst—including those in our own affluent neighborhoods, at our workplaces, or in our schools.

Perhaps once we have met the poor in the obvious places, such as the Downtown Eastside or on a short-term mission trip to Cambodia, we will have eyes to see the poor in our own neighborhoods, because the struggling are found across every sector of society. Some who are affluent are unable to feed themselves, such as the disabled, the mentally ill, the elderly, or those suffering from other infirmities. Both rich and poor are imprisoned by addictions and need the freedom that Jesus offers.

Interestingly, in Matthew 25, Jesus does not categorize people based on class (rich or poor, peasant or scribe), but rather identifies those whose needs are unmet: *I was hungry. I was thirsty. I was unclothed. I was in prison. I was sick.* Ultimately, we will be called to account for how we treated the "least," and not everyone who struggles is economically poor.

So many needs surround us. As we seek to follow the way of Jesus, we need to ask him to renew our minds and hearts continually so that we will see those who are suffering or struggling. We must be able to respond with compassion and love.

Mutuality

Down the street from our house, at the corner of the block, was a big gravel car park. On one side loomed an old factory with no windows, giving it an Eastern European, Communist bloc feel. A huge billboard rose from the middle of the lot, advertising products to people with no money. Apart from an occasional car and a few used needles discarded by drug users, the lot was usually empty.

Day after day, as we walked by that abandoned lot filled with cracked concrete and trash, we dreamed of nurturing something more. Something beautiful and lush. Something whimsical and nourishing. So I went to City Hall and paid my money to a lady, who waved me over to an ancient computer, where I found the name of the owners of the windowless factory and the empty lot: Wing Wing Chinese Sausage Factory. Then I knocked at the door of Wing Wing Chinese Sausage Factory and asked, "Can we turn your parking lot into a public garden?"

I didn't ask about the box planters. Nor did I mention that we'd be inviting our homeless neighbors to get their hands dirty. But of course, that's what we were thinking.

When the owners of Wing Wing said yes, I choked back my surprise. Then I trotted home and announced the good news to everyone: "We've got it. The parking lot is ours to turn into a community garden!"

Those first few months were a rush of enthusiasm. We'd barely started, but strangers gave us thumbs-up. Passersby threw out compliments. Addicts stumbled by with cheery greetings. Others came in to help or give advice, move soil or build boxes. But most of all, people came to plant things. To give birth to life.

An elderly Korean lady from across the road planted spinach and Asian herbs. The aboriginal housing block next door sent their troubled youth to work out their frustration with rakes and hoes. They mixed it up with the Hispanic community group from down the road, who grew food for their weekly lunches.

One day, a few of us were gathered to eat ice cream in the garden when a homeless man wandered in and asked if he could plant one seedling. He knelt down and carefully placed the little green sprig of life into the dark soil, then looked up at us with pride and asked if he could mark it as his own. Two-year-old Lily offered up her popsicle stick, and we wrote his name on it, inserting it into the soil beside his tiny plant.

That day, we birthed not only a seedling but also an idea: the popsicle stick garden. From that day onward, whenever someone came by wanting to plant a tiny seed or plant—their contribution to the beautiful jungle on the corner—we gave them a popsicle stick with their name, so they could mark their tiny little piece of paradise.

Later that summer, we gathered to enjoy the setting sun. Some of us climbed up on the still-looming billboard and set up a movie projector with speakers. We sat on old plastic crates around the garden and ate popcorn, enjoying a movie projected on the wall of the Wing Wing Chinese Sausage Factory.

Home to more than cars and advertisements, the popsicle stick garden became a gathering place for life and laughter and the joy of being together in the dirty soil that gives birth to life. But if someone from out of town had come and set up that garden for us, it would not have transformed our lives, let alone our neighbors. As Jesus showed us in his life and ministry, healing and transformation flow out of relationship—not the delivery of services.

True love flows out of mutuality, where we blur the lines between those who are serving and those who are receiving, and where we humbly acknowledge that we all have something to offer and something to receive from one another. If you teach me what you know about gardening, I'll share the weeding workload with you. Such relationships of mutuality empower the poor, whereas one-way acts of benevolence may disempower them.[66]

In soup kitchens, when church volunteers take up a post in the kitchen, they often leave feeling good about themselves and their benevolence. And though the poor might be amply fed after shuffling through for their meals, they usually leave feeling as lonely and alienated as ever. As Christians, we have become so fixated on our roles as servants that we miss out on the relationships of mutuality that the Spirit wants to knit between people.

Jesus knew the power of blurred lines and introduced it to his disciples in the practice of foot washing. When Jesus goes to wash Peter's feet, Peter refuses, and Jesus rebukes him: "Unless I wash you, you have no part with me." He goes on to challenge the whole group: "Now that I, your Lord and Teacher, have washed your feet, you also should wash one another's feet. I have set you an example that you should do as I have done for you . . . Now that you know these things, you will be blessed if you do them."[67]

This is a beautiful picture of mutuality. Not one person greedily insists on doing all the foot washing so that they might have the glory, but rather each one is invited to participate by serving the others. When we allow those we have labeled victims or the poor to serve and participate in our acts of transforming love, we usher in the kingdom of God.

Community

One night, we gathered in our home for a Bible study about love: love is patient, love is kind, love is long-suffering, that kind of thing. There were some new friends from the street with us, and I hoped they would hear about love and want to know more about God.

Patrick had come to our house like a lost boy from never-never land. With his long, black, dreadlocked hair bundled inside a red, yellow, and green beanie, I took him for a Rastafarian at first—and indeed, he refused to eat meat, saying he was a vegan. Innocent to the streets and the drugs that made this neighborhood go round, Patrick viewed the world through wide eyes and seemed to be looking for a haven. I hoped he'd find it in our living room that night.

When the Bible study started, Beth spoke. Whenever Beth came by our house in her bulky winter coat, she'd flash her toothless grin and wrap me in a warm bear hug. "My sista from another mista," I'd say, even though she was probably twenty years older. And she would always counter with a punch on my arm. "My brotha from anotha mudda." Though she stood a full foot shorter than me, even with her curly Afro, her presence in the room was mighty. And that night, it was mightier than usual.

She talked of the love she felt for the young girl lying drugged in the alleyway. She talked about scolding the pimps and the abusers. She was like a miniature Martin Luther King Jr. with a lisp—feisty and not afraid of the Big Bad Wolf. My mind wandered to an image of the pimp she was referring to: a giant dude standing on the corner, overseeing his girls, ready to bite if they stepped out of line.

Still, Beth talked. I glanced at my watch and noticed that the time had come to wrap things up. Then Beth launched into another story about her love for another desperate young woman on the street. I groaned inwardly. Time's a tickin'.

Love is patient. The words floated into my mind. *Love is kind. Yeah, yeah, I know. Hilarious, God—good one! Love is long-suffering.* Here I was, stuck in an object lesson of my own making, with God having a great big chuckle.

When Beth finally stopped talking, I gave her another bear hug. "My sista, thanks for teaching us about love and patience and long-suffering."

"You got it, brotha," she lisped, then launched into her raucous laugh.

Throughout Beth's monologue, Patrick had been quiet, but as our meeting devolved into laughter and chatter, I saw him huddled in the corner with our roommate Justin, poring over Justin's Bible. And I knew they were talking about God's love.

When we try to describe the love of God in words, it's like listening to a street preacher talk about salvation. Our words can rarely speak as powerfully as the lives we live together, so when people get together and create a space of welcome for others, the Spirit moves, and everyone experiences the love of God embodied. This is especially magical for those who are used to being excluded, rather than welcomed.

It is the radical welcome of Christ with skin on.

—— CHAPTER 9 ——

SUBVERSIVE
CITIZENSHIP

> Justice is what love looks like in public.
> —CORNEL WEST

Over time, the gatherings in our home grew larger. Community dinners around our table overflowed with people—poor friends from the streets enjoying fellowship with rich friends from affluent suburbs. And as our table extended, we became increasingly aware that our battles were not against flesh and blood, but against powers and principalities, the systems and structures that hold people captive. As a community, we felt called to go deeper in our pursuit of biblical justice.

That summer we organized a justice festival in a field on the outskirts of the city, inviting our friends from the Downtown Eastside to gather with other followers of Jesus who cared about justice and music and creativity. We planned for about two hundred people, but more than six hundred showed up to camp in tents and sit around on hay bales. We listened to bands play and shared stories of transformation and teaching about the kingdom. It was a picture of heaven on earth.

But we knew that we wanted our pursuit of justice to be more than an inspiring annual event, so we began to gather after dinner on Tuesday nights to dream about disrupting injustice in the tradition of Jesus and the prophets of old. We dubbed our gatherings Creative World Justice.

Together, we studied the street theater and dramatic antics of biblical prophets, such as Isaiah and Micah, who went around naked to convey their messages—the first nudists for justice![68] We also studied Jeremiah, who buried his linen underpants under a rock thirteen hundred miles away from Jerusalem as a symbolic gesture.[69] As we immersed ourselves in the story of John the Baptist, we counted the cost of speaking the truth to those in power.[70] And when we read about how Jesus instructed his disciples to shake the dust off their feet, we talked about how it was a public and symbolic statement of resistance.[71]

The more we studied Scripture, the more we saw that the prophets spoke time and time again to those in power of God's heart for the poor. The call for justice was central to a true prophet's message:

> *Amos the prophet:* "Hear this, you who trample the needy and do away with the poor of the land!"[72]
> *Isaiah the prophet:* "Seek justice. Defend the oppressed. Take up the cause of the fatherless; plead the case of the widow."[73]
> *Jeremiah the prophet:* "Woe to him who builds his palace by unrighteousness, his upper rooms by injustice."[74]

Ezekiel the prophet: "Now this was the sin of your sister Sodom: She and her daughters were arrogant, overfed and unconcerned; they did not help the poor and needy."[75]
Micah the prophet: "He has shown you, O mortal, what is good. And what does the LORD require of you? To act justly and to love mercy and to walk humbly with your God."[76]
Zechariah the prophet: "This is what the LORD Almighty said: . . . 'Do not oppress the widow or the fatherless, the foreigner or the poor.'"[77]

In the few churches still recognizing the role of prophets today (mostly Pentecostal and charismatic churches), the focus has strayed far from the biblical call to justice. These modern-day prophets mostly offer warm and fuzzy future predictions about what an individual will do in his or her ministry or career. Sadly, the call to repent for ignoring the poor or living affluent lifestyles in a world of poverty has mostly been lost.

Historically, there were always false prophets who spoke only positive, uplifting words that people loved to hear, such as "You will do great things!" or "Your ministry is going to have a huge impact!" or "God is going to bless you with prosperity!" And these prophets feasted at the king's table, while the truth-telling prophets were exiled to the caves outside.[78]

As we read the Gospels, we were convicted by how Jesus never held back when speaking to the powerful. The religious leaders in particular received harsh critique for their unjust practices: "Woe to you Pharisees, because you give God a tenth of your mint, rue and all other kinds of garden herbs, but you neglect justice and the love of God."[79]

We prayed that God would help us to repent of our comfort, and give us the courage to be truth-telling prophets of love, kindness, and justice, calling people to remember the poor.

Hoping to learn more about the biblical vision of justice, I invited our friend Dave, an activist and respected Old Testament scholar and professor, to teach us about how we might move away from the status quo and toward the hope of God's justice. While teaching in Israel, Dave had been deeply moved by the suffering of the Palestinians. When he returned to Canada, he pulled back from teaching theology to begin organizing for justice on the streets of Vancouver. I respected his integrity and the price he was willing to pay to pursue Jesus' upside-down kingdom on earth.

Wearing his trademark baseball cap, and with his hands stuffed in a hoodie for warmth, Dave taught our little group about three phases of biblical justice. First, in *solidarity*, we tie our well-being to the well-being of those God leans toward—the poor. Next, we enter a season of *resistance* together, and as we are inspired by the Spirit, we speak truth to power and take symbolic actions to highlight injustice and ask for change. Finally, by God's grace, we long to reach the place of *liberation*, where both the oppressed and the oppressors are transformed when they open themselves to the work of God.

With Dave's helpful framework stirring our imaginations, we were ready to begin practicing prophetic justice.

Solidarity

Along with our friends who lived on the streets, some of those gathering around our table were recent immigrants who were seeking asylum in Canada.

One night, a young man from Indonesia shared about his experience as a cruise ship worker, where the lowest-paid workers receive as little as $45 a month for working seven days a week and twenty hours a day, in breach of their contracts.

As he told his story, my mind went back to our years living in developing world slums, when I knew mothers and fathers, sons and daughters who would have accepted such conditions willingly because their families were living in such desperate poverty. In such circumstances, the poor become vulnerable to exploitation and are willing to sacrifice their well-being to help their families.

For those of us who come from positions of privilege, it can be easy to assume that because no one is holding a gun to these workers' heads, they are not being exploited by their employers. Some might argue that they are free to accept these positions, or not.

But if the kingdom of God is going to come to earth, we need to speak up for those who are being exploited because they lack choices. Even better, we need to amplify the voices of the oppressed so that others can hear their stories. We can use our liberty and privilege to benefit those who lack such freedom and power.

We could not easily forget our Indonesian friend's story, because every summer, dozens of cruise ships carrying more than eight hundred thousand passengers annually docked just blocks away from our Vancouver home. We began to do more research on the cruise ship industry and to film interviews with cruise ship workers. As we prayed and brainstormed, we felt that joy and love, creativity and music were more likely to bring change than angry marches. So we got busy dreaming, organizing, and praying.

Resistance

Dressed in tight striped pants, knee-high leather boots, and a flowing white blouse, I leaped onto an overturned bucket and snarled, "Ahoy, there, all ye pirates of justice!" into a megaphone, in my best Blackbeard voice.

Lacking significant chest hair, I had drawn some on my chest with a marker. I wanted to be a pirate, after all, not a cabin boy! I tossed my long, curly hair back dramatically, and it rattled with ribbons and beads. Whoever said you can't have fun when you're fighting for justice?

A crowd of tourists milled around with bemused smiles and poised cameras, watching as our raucous crowd of 120 pirates swayed and sashayed to the music of our joyful minstrels. The Pirate Flash Mob, organized through Facebook and planned over meals and meetings in our little home, wove its way around the dock of Canada Place in downtown Vancouver. We sang merrily and waved our homemade black Jolly Roger flag.

Ruth, our usually quiet community member, danced forward and placed a wooden board between a couple of buckets, thus constructing our makeshift pirate plank.

"It's time to take some prisoners! Arrrrrr, yes! It's time to make 'em walk the plank! Death to exploitation!" I barked.

"Aaaarrrrrrr," growled the crowd exuberantly.

A young wench wearing a bandana and striped T-shirt stepped forward, and Jason fastened a black strip of cloth around her head. The word exploitation was scrawled in white paint upon the cloth. In real life, this first-time protestor was a social work student who had recently begun attending our gatherings. She stepped tentatively onto the plank and wobbled her way across, barely a foot off the ground. As her toes touched down at the end, the crowd roared its approval with jeers and whoops.

"Death to 'No Days Off'! Walk the plank!"

My son Jayden danced forward with excitement. He was dressed as a cabin boy with a three-cornered hat, an eye patch, and a "No Days Off" blindfold around his eyes. He edged across the plank, spurred on by rowdy shouts of approval.

We continued in this manner until it seemed right to make a rousing pirate speech. I stepped onto one of the buckets and brought the loudspeaker to my painted lips.

"Ahoy, there, pirates! Ye listen to me! This here cruise ship . . ." I gestured dramatically behind me to the massive hull of the floating pride of Carnival's cruise line. "This here cruise ship be sailing the seven seas, exploitin' and pillagin' and plunderin' its workers. They be workin' seven days a week, for months on end. And some o' dem be getting paid as little as $45 a month!"

What I lacked in an authentic accent, I more than made up for in flamboyant gestures. The enthusiastic crowd responded with hoots and howls.

Buoyed by the turnout and energized by the passion of the protestors, local TV crews filmed the proceedings and journalists jotted notes in little books.

When the crowd began to disperse, my mind ran to our inspiration: Jesus, who came in the long-lost tradition of the gnarly prophets of old. Wild. Creative. Provocative. Imaginative. Subversive.

But how far would we be willing to go in the pursuit of justice?

Sometimes, Good People
Need to Break Bad Laws

Followers of Jesus have a rich history of protest and civil disobedience. Historically, we have been closer to pirates and prophets—pushed to the edges of society, maligned and abused—than upstanding, respectable citizens.

The law cannot be our ultimate moral guide. Slavery was lawful. The Holocaust was legal. Segregation was legally sanctioned. As Howard Zinn reminds us, "Historically, the most terrible things—war, genocide and slavery—have resulted not from disobedience, but from obedience."[80] Simply put, the law does not dictate our ethics. God does. So it should not surprise us that the One we follow was executed as a criminal, and that there will be times when we are called to break unjust laws ourselves.

Those who stand in solidarity with people on the margins of society are much more likely to find themselves standing up against unjust laws, because they know how such laws affect their friends, the poor.

As far back as the book of Exodus, the Hebrew midwives refused to carry out the Pharaoh's repugnant order to murder newborn babies.

The first people who sought to worship Jesus, a trio of spiritual gurus from Asia, deliberately disobeyed the orders of King Herod and refused to go back and tell the authorities where Jesus and his parents were camping out. This was a criminal offense punishable by death, the first recorded act of civil disobedience in the New Testament.

At the end of his life, Jesus faced execution as a common criminal, or the Roman version of an electric chair, because his subversive presence in first-century Palestine threatened the empire. And what's more, he expected his followers to carry on in his footsteps. Almost all of his disciples went on to be executed or imprisoned for their faith. And he promised us that when, not if, we were arrested, the Holy Spirit would give us the words to say.[81]

But Jesus did not come to overthrow the government, nor to get Christian politicians elected into power, nor to establish a "Christian" empire brought about by force, strength, and political influence. Instead, Jesus wanted us to imagine a different kind of revolution—a gentle, subversive revolution of love, courage, justice, and kindness to the people least likely to be offered that kindness.

If Jesus inspired civil disobedience at the beginning of his life and ended up being killed by the political system that he criticized, we must consider what happened between his birth and death that so threatened the powers.

While the Romans held the reins of political power in first-century Judea, they counted on local Jewish authorities, the priests and other religious leaders, to maintain public order. These religious leaders had no love for the Roman Empire, but they benefited from the system. They were a bit like the Taliban—extremely religious, with political power to back up their agenda.

Then Jesus, a subversive teacher, prophet, and healer, came into the temple. He flouted their religious purity laws and criticized their temple taxes because he saw how they oppressed the people.

One Sabbath, Jesus entered the synagogue and met a man with a shriveled hand. The religious authorities had been hoping to accuse Jesus, so they watched him closely to see if he would illegally heal the man.

Jesus said to the man with the shriveled hand, "Stand up in front of everyone." Clearly, Jesus had mercy and compassion on the man and wanted to heal him. But why didn't he just quietly usher him into a side room and heal him there? Was it really necessary to provoke the ire of the authorities by calling the man to stand before everyone?

Then, to make matters worse, Jesus challenged the interpretation of the Sabbath law, which had been twisted to benefit the wealthy and to disregard the needs of the poor and sick. Seeking to undermine the status quo, Jesus asked the temple authorities, "Which is lawful on the Sabbath: to do good or to do evil, to save life or to kill?"

But the leaders remained silent. And Jesus "looked around at them in anger and, deeply distressed at their stubborn hearts, said to the man, 'Stretch out your hand.' He stretched it out, and his hand was completely restored. Then the Pharisees went out and began to plot with the Herodians how they might kill Jesus."[82]

The Gospels reveal to us that Jesus walked from Galilee to Jerusalem on what could be seen as a nonviolent protest march. More than a millennium later, Gandhi, inspired by Jesus, walked to Dandi on his famous salt march protesting unjust taxation by the British. And later still, Martin Luther King Jr., at the time a twenty-seven-year-old pastor of a small Baptist church, walked from Selma to Montgomery, Alabama, to protest the city's racial segregation laws and to initiate the bus boycott sparked by Rosa Parks's arrest for refusing to give up her seat to a white man.

When Jesus arrived in Jerusalem, he entered the temple,

where the religious leaders worked in complicity with the Roman Empire by forcing the poor to pay exorbitant fees to worship God. Jesus then engaged in what I would call nonviolent direct action. He made a whip and drove the animals out of the temple courts, pushing over tables and strewing coins everywhere. One thing is for certain: nonviolent does not mean passive!

As we sat in the safety and comfort of our living room week after week discussing injustice and searching the Scriptures, we realized that Jesus was calling us farther along the justice road. It wasn't enough for us to feel solidarity for the poor, nor to engage in creative acts of resistance. We realized that we could not follow the footsteps of Jesus without coming into conflict with the world system.

As Father John Dear writes of Jesus, "He did not hit anyone, hurt anyone, kill anyone, or drop any bombs—but he was not passive. He was active, provocative, dangerous, illegal, and civilly disobedient, a disturber of the peace, a troublemaker, a nonviolent revolutionary who broke the unjust laws and mores of an unjust society." Father John Dear, himself jailed multiple times for taking action against military installations, jokingly calls Jesus "a one man crime wave."[83]

Our little band of Pirates of Justice might not have brought about the eradication of unjust labor practices, but we were inviting people to step out of their comfort zones and take tiny steps toward Jesus and his subversive, costly ways. We also knew that such steps might provoke the ire of the empire, and we might face disapproval from our churches and families as we sought to open ourselves to the work of God in the world. We sought transformation for ourselves and transformation for the oppressed of the world.

Liberation

A few weeks after our Pirates of Justice debut, I received an email from an American dancer named Jessica. She was working on the Holland America cruise ships line, and she had heard about the flash mob through media reports and wanted to let us know that the conditions on her cruise ship were exactly as we had described them. While her own pay and conditions as a North American were more than generous, a little digging and getting to know shipmates from poorer countries (such as the Philippines) revealed that some were working in slavelike conditions, especially those occupying the lowliest jobs on the ship.

Jessica indicated that she was willing to do anything, even endanger her employment or break the contract she had signed (effectively breaking the law), to help bring attention to the situation. I worried for her safety, but I knew she had made her decision to stand with those who were being exploited.

When God's law of compassion and justice comes into conflict with our human laws, Christians are faced with a dilemma. But as St. Augustine said, "An unjust law is no law at all." And those who stand alongside the poor on the margins of society will inevitably witness more injustice than others, because such laws are often made to protect the interests of the rich and powerful.

So what should our response be? How can we speak out a holy no to the authorities who are standing on the heads of the poor? According to the *Washington Post*, an estimated 12,000 lobbyists hired by corporations and wealthy interest groups try to influence legislation, resulting in a multibillion-dollar industry.[84] I believe there is a biblical mandate for Christ-followers to become lobbyists for the poor.

Ron Sider asks why "we think it is more spiritual to operate 'ambulances' which pick up the bloody victims of destructive social structures rather than trying to change the structures themselves"?[85] Though we honor those who become missionaries to serve the exploited families of Filipino slums, we often consider it unacceptable or unchristian to challenge the systems and structures that exploited them in the first place.

In contrast, Jesus regularly engaged in acts of blatant civil disobedience that disrupted injustice and challenged the status quo. Such acts brought Jesus and his followers into conflict with the law enforcers of the land. In Luke 13, Jesus healed a crippled woman on the Sabbath.[86] In Luke 14, Jesus healed a man from dropsy on the Sabbath.[87] In John 5, Jesus healed a lame man at the pool of Bethesda on the Sabbath.[88] In multiple instances, Jesus associated with unclean people whom religious law required him to avoid—such as sinners, lepers, Samaritan women, and tax collectors. In Matthew 15, the disciples broke the laws of ritual washing, and Jesus calls the religious leaders hypocrites.[89] In Matthew 12, the disciples pick grain to eat on the Sabbath, and Jesus defends their actions on the grounds that the needs of hunger outweigh legal strictures.[90] And in Matthew 21, Jesus clears the temple of exploitative money changers.[91]

Jessica's courage inspired me and reminded me of the boldness of Jesus. Together, we hatched a plan to smuggle disposable cameras into the hands of her shipmates so they could share their stories with a wider audience. Though Jessica was worried about getting caught, I knew she wouldn't back down.

As the weeks turned into months, we whipped up more media interest and connected journalists to Jessica by phone while she was on board a cruise ship off the coast of Brazil. I prayed no one in the cruise line business would recognize her voice on the radio!

Eventually, we received a series of simple photos of potato peelers, laundrymen, cleaners, and cooks, as well as their lodgings. Each image told a story. Ruth and others in our community used their artistic skills to juxtapose these photos with photos of opulence and luxury used in cruise line advertising. Simple facts and figures completed the exhibition, and it was shown all over Vancouver.

After Jesus was executed and then resurrected, Peter and John were ordered by the local authorities not to speak about the alternative kingdom that Jesus was ushering in. But they refused, saying, "Which is right in God's eyes: to listen to you, or to him? You be the judges! As for us, we cannot help speaking about what we have seen and heard."[92] If their preaching had been harmless advice encouraging people to be nice to each other, they would not have been thrown in prison. But Jesus' vision of the kingdom of God was a threat to the empire.

In the same way, Jessica refused to be silent about the injustice she saw and the hope she had for an alternative way of offering fair wages and working conditions to the poor. She was inspired by the words of Isaiah 58, where God's light shines forth because godly people refuse to allow the exploitation of workers. In fact, Isaiah 58 teaches us that worship without justice is repulsive in God's eyes.

To Submit Is Not Always to Obey

After Jesus' death and resurrection, King Herod arrested some of the believers, including James and Peter, and put them on public trial. The night before the trial, an angel of the Lord woke Peter up, removed his chains, opened the prison doors, and led him out the main gate of the prison. Though Peter left the prison, James was executed. Like Jesus, some may be called to pay the ultimate price for justice.

Yet after escaping from jail, where he had been imprisoned for breaking the law, Peter went on to write in a letter: "Submit yourselves for the Lord's sake to every authority: whether to the emperor, as the supreme authority, or to governors, who are sent by him to punish those who do wrong and to commend those who do right. For it is God's will that by doing good you should silence the ignorant talk of foolish people."[93]

Similarly, while Paul was in Damascus, he escaped from a city governor who was trying to arrest him. He concealed himself in a basket and had himself lowered down the city wall through a window. Then after reaching safety, he wrote in a letter, "Let everyone be subject to the governing authorities, for there is no authority except that which God has established. The authorities that exist have been established by God. Consequently, whoever rebels against the authority is rebelling against what God has instituted, and those who do so will bring judgment on themselves."[94]

So are Peter and Paul hypocrites, asking followers to do as they say but not as they do? Though these passages have been used to maintain the status quo ever since the Emperor Constantine became a Christian and made it the official religion of the empire, there is an obvious disconnect between Peter's and Paul's actions and the way we have traditionally interpreted their words.

The problem is in the way these passages have been translated. The Greek word *hupotasso*, which has been translated as "submit" or "be subject," literally means to arrange in an orderly manner underneath. Original readers would have understood it this way, but the meaning is obscured in our English translation. This word is used in Ephesians 5:22 to encourage husbands and wives to submit to one another, and it reflects God's concern for order. Thus, governing authorities are necessary for keeping the peace.

In contrast, *hupokouo*, which is best translated as "obey," literally means to conform, to hearken to a command, or to kowtow to an authority as a subordinate. Used twenty-one times in the New Testament, this word always connotes a hierarchical context, as in the relationship between children and their parents or slaves and their masters.[95]

In the New Testament Greek, to submit does *not* always mean to obey!

Though Paul, Peter, and other followers of Jesus deliberately broke laws that were in conflict with God's commands, they still submitted to the authorities by accepting the legal consequences of their actions; so if we break an unjust law to highlight and protest its injustice, we must be willing to submit to the punishment for breaking such laws in order to demonstrate our respect for the rule of law in general.

Jesus himself challenged the powers, but he submitted to the law of the land when those powers chose to execute him. He did not raise up an army of angels to overcome them because he refused to use their military methods.

And so must we, as followers of Christ, stand up with a holy no as we walk the justice road of transformation and liberation. In humble submission to the government, we must also be ready to accept the consequences of our actions, which may include imprisonment or even death.

Loose the Chains of Injustice

These thoughts about submission and obedience were running through my mind as I gathered with about a dozen others from our community outside the Singaporean Embassy in downtown Vancouver. Draped over our shoulders and wrapped around our arms and legs were heavy metal chains.

Singapore is an affluent nation in the middle of a sea of poverty. Neighboring countries such as Indonesia, Burma, Sri Lanka, Cambodia, and the Philippines send roughly 170,000 impoverished young women to Singapore every year to work as domestic maids. Yet the Singaporean government has refused to guarantee these vulnerable foreign women a weekly day off by law, even though all other Singaporean employees receive a mandated day off.

In Hong Kong, there is a similar migrant situation, but their law ensures one day off every week. As a result, according to Human Rights Watch, Hong Kong maids suffer fewer than a third of the number of deaths by workplace "accident" or suicide (most by jumping or falling from residential buildings) than maids in Singapore.

For several years, this situation had been troubling me. I didn't want to take this issue on because my parents lived in Singapore, and I knew dozens of maids and counted a lot of their employers as my friends. I didn't want to alienate my Singaporean friends, and I certainly didn't want to get banned from Singapore and be unable to visit my parents.

So I wrestled with God in prayer, taking a week to fast and to ask God to raise up someone else. I was not a Singaporean, and I wasn't sure how the embassy officials would receive this message from me, an ignorant *Ang Mo* foreigner. After my week of prayer and fasting, I still felt compelled to stand up for these women.

One night at a gathering in our home, I shared the words of Aung San Suu Kyi, the Burmese democracy leader who was imprisoned for many years, who said, "Use your liberty to promote ours." Her words had shown me that rather than wringing my hands and feeling guilty about my privilege, I needed to recognize its existence, acknowledge that it would not go away, and then figure out how best to use it for others. I pointed out that most of us in the West are blessed with freedom of speech and liberty to speak up for those who have been silenced around the world. In Vancouver, I figured we would be able to get away with a sharper criticism of the Singaporean government than someone in Singapore, where protest is tightly regulated.

Together, we decided to gather at Singaporean embassies in Vancouver and Washington, DC. (Some friends there gamely agreed to join us in what we hyped up as a "simultaneous multicity protest.") Some of us were dressed as maids with mops, brooms, and other cleaning implements. Others were dressed in suits and ties. All of us were bound by heavy metal chains to represent the bondage that comes to rich and poor alike through injustice. Our simple request was for the Singaporean government to change the law to ensure that these maids were given one day of rest each week, as recommended by the biblical provisions of the fourth commandment and as adopted by most developed governments of the world.

Our presence that day was more awkward than controversial. We were not arrested, and the consulate workers did their best to ignore us. The media came, there was a little TV and newspaper coverage, and not much seemed to change.

Many will seek to judge our actions by their effectiveness. Did the Singaporean government change the law to ensure a day off for maids? Yes, they did—partially, the following year—but that decision likely had nothing to do with us!

The words of the prophets usually fell on deaf ears. If we measure the prophetic actions and statements of Amos, Isaiah, Micah, Jeremiah, and the others by the standards of the world, they were mostly wasted efforts. Awkward acts with little fruit.

But in the economy of Jesus' upside-down kingdom, no act of solidarity with the poor and the marginalized is ever wasted. For he calls us to faithfulness, not success.

CHAPTER 10

SUBVERSIVE
SUFFERING

> Faith begins at the point where atheists
> suppose that it must be at an end . . . with
> the bleakness and power which is the night
> of the cross.
>
> —MIROSLAV VOLF

Most of us won't have the chance to lay down our lives in a blaze of glory. But all of us are invited to lay down our lives daily through tiny moments of joyful obedience.

Along with Jason and his new wife Laura, I took the 105 bus from London's Heathrow Airport to Southall, a vibrant Indian community on the outskirts of London. We had come to England to offer training on ministry among the urban poor. Jason and Laura, who was pregnant with their first baby, were excited to be taking one last trip overseas before the demands of parenthood would make travel more difficult.

As we disembarked from the bus, our senses were overwhelmed by an intense onslaught of colors and smells—exotic saris, delicious Indian sweets, bustling crowds. The only incongruity was the bitterly cold British weather.

We were warmly welcomed by Helen Sidebotham, a co-leader of Servants to Asia's Urban Poor and a dear friend from many years back. Helen was thin with pale white British skin and red hair. She looked distinctly out of place in this majority Indian neighborhood, but she greeted us cheerfully, explaining the context: "This is the first bus stop from Heathrow Airport, so a lot of refugees and asylum seekers have ended up here. In fact, most of the pubs here accept Indian rupees as legal currency!"

We laughed and soaked it all in. As we made our way to the training center, Laura cradled her belly, looking uncomfortable.

The next morning, Jason told me that Laura wasn't feeling well and wouldn't be able to teach her session that day. A doctor herself, Laura felt that something was not right with the baby. We prayed together, and Jason took his wife to the hospital.

When Jason called later that day, I knew from his trembling voice what he was going to say. My heart sank. The agonized words caught in Jason's throat. "Laura has miscarried . . . we've lost the baby."

The Night Closes In

A couple of days later, I had to travel outside London for another training session. With instructions on how to take London's Underground train, I set out alone, grateful for the long journey that would give me time to think, pray, and grieve for my dear friends. I felt particularly heavy and stressed that day.

Built more than 150 years ago, the Tube is a marvel of human engineering that runs sixty meters (two hundred feet) below the surface of the earth in some places. As the packed train rumbled through these subterranean tunnels, I tried to carve out some personal space amid the other passengers. During rush hour, the Waterloo station alone serves upward of 57,000 passengers, and it felt like every single one of them had managed to squeeze into my train. The air felt heavy with the sickly smell of wet winter clothing.

A subtle change in the sound of the train's engine alerted me that something was wrong, and my fears were confirmed when the train ground to a halt. Quiet descended on the cabin. Some passengers shuffled their newspapers or sighed impatiently. Others looked bored or rolled their eyes in frustration.

I tore off my restrictive jacket, hoping to relieve the uneasy feeling that the walls were closing in around me. I unwrapped my scarf and let it fall to the floor, then loosened my collar and used my elbows to pry a few more inches of space from those around me. But nothing helped the sickening dread I felt rising within my upper stomach. I fought the urge to claw at the walls and searched frantically for a way out of the train.

But the walls of the tunnel were mere inches from the glass windows of the train, so there was no escape, either through a window or by prying open a door. As the long minutes of waiting ticked by, I began to panic as I thought about how long we might be stuck in that packed metal capsule underneath the earth, where the air seemed to be in desperately short supply.

Finally, after what seemed like an eternity, when I didn't think I could bear even one more second, the train heaved forward and began rolling toward our destination. Involuntary, I shouted, "Praise the Lord God Almighty!" The other passengers turned and looked at me, obviously amused.

That was my first experience with such anxiety, but ever since, I have struggled with chronic claustrophobia.

Later that week, I shocked myself by bursting into tears as I struggled to get on the plane to return to Vancouver. I ended up missing my flight. The next day, heavily drugged but still trembling with fear, I boarded a plane, desperate to see Nay and the kids.

Back in Vancouver, buses and trains became places of increasing anxiety. I could not get into elevators and feared I might never fly again. My doctor prescribed pills, and caring Christian friends prayed for me. For several months, I met with a psychologist once a week, but nothing seemed to help. For the first time in my life, I felt fragile as my sense of invincibility and self-confidence evaporated.

I remembered all the times I had been impatient with Nay and others for their fears and anxieties. *Oh, you're scared to come to the inner city?* I'd thought. *Well, toughen up! Relax!* I had been such a callous fool, and now I worried that my fear would overwhelm me.

I asked God to take this thorn away, but it remained firmly lodged in my side.

Finding Light in the Darkness

As I struggled to find healing, my friend Scott Bessenecker told me about his recent retreat at a Benedictine monastery. While sitting and praying, staring absentmindedly at a noxious weed known as Creeping Charlie, he sensed God telling him to take some of that weed and plant it in his garden at home.

Scott thought this was pretty strange, but he dutifully dug up a vibrant patch of Creeping Charlie and transplanted it into his garden when he got home. He even added topsoil and fertilizer. A day or so later, Scott came to tend his Creeping Charlie, and it was dead.

He tried it again, this time trying to care for it a little better. Within days, the weed had shriveled and died.

On the third attempt, Scott cleared away all the surrounding plants to make a little path for the Creeping Charlie through the middle of his garden. But strangely enough, the very thing that others could not get out of their lawns would not grow in his garden.

As he reflected on the experiment, Scott heard God saying, *This weed won't grow in a healthy garden.*

God spoke poignantly to me through Scott's prophetic and obedient action. I realized that I was trying to get rid of the weed of claustrophobia in my life by dousing it with spiritual weed killers: healing prayer, counseling, systematic desensitization, cognitive behavioral therapy. You name it, I tried it. But the weed just kept coming back.

Scott's story reminded me that God wanted me to spend more energy developing a healthy garden, where such a noxious weed could not grow.

During this time of struggle, the daily prayer rhythms that our community had developed over the previous few years became more and more critical to my well-being. Mornings and evenings, our community gathered to pray, reflect, sing psalms, and sit in God's presence in silence. When I did not have the strength to turn to God on my own, these communal practices carried me forward.

Gradually, I learned that the harder I fought my anxieties, the worse they got. The more I resisted my fears, the greater power I gave them. Perhaps this is what Jesus meant when he said, "If anyone slaps you on the right cheek, turn to them the other cheek also."[96] For when we try to fight demons, we empower them.

We had first learned this principle from our friends in Cambodia, who often seemed passive in the face of evil. But they knew that it is only when you flow with the enemy that you can overcome the enemy.

We had also seen this with our friends struggling with addiction. When they focused solely on the drugs and over-coming their addictions, they became even more mired in the obsession. But when they focused on what was life-giving and good, holy and beautiful, their need for drugs eventually faded away.

As Anthony de Mello writes, "How does one cope with evil? Not by fighting it but by understanding it. In under-standing, it disappears. How does one cope with darkness? Not with one's fist. You don't chase darkness out of the room with a broom, you turn on a light. The more you fight darkness, the more real it becomes to you, and the more you exhaust yourself. But when you turn on the light of aware-ness, it melts."[97]

As I came to terms with the fact that my claustrophobia could not be overcome, I began trying to understand it, to pur-sue a life-giving opposite. For me, there was only one thing that would get me on a plane, and that was the possibility that my small amount of suffering and anxiety—the psy-chological cost of taking that flight—might help relieve the suffering of others. Only love could conquer my fear.

When I focused on the purpose and calling God had given me to serve the poor, I was able to summon up the courage to think about flying again.

But God wasn't finished with me yet. There would be more purifying to come.

The Night of the Cross

My physician sat behind a big desk, shuffling through a pile of test results. Looking up at me, his eyes creased with compassion, he said, "You have cancer. We're going to have to operate immediately to remove your whole colon before the cancer spreads any further. At that point, we'll know how far it has developed."

As I tried to understand what he was saying, tears welled up and dark thoughts flew through my head.

Was I going to die? Would Jayden and Micah be orphaned? Would Nay be left a widow? How would I function without a colon? *Lord, I'm not even forty—barely halfway through my life.*

I fled home, reeling from the shock, and fell into Nay's embrace.

Within a couple of weeks, I was on the operating table, thanks to the machinery of the Canadian health system. During my recovery, my surgeon—a breezy, efficient older man—rushed into the room and out again to his next appointment, leaving me alone and with unasked questions on my lips.

Somehow Nay juggled the kids and cared for me, visiting the hospital each day as my recovery dragged on for weeks, set back by one complication after another.

As I suffered in this pit of despair, I found comfort in the writings of people of faith. Father Richard Rohr writes, "Pain teaches a most counterintuitive thing—that we must go down before we even know what up is. In terms of the ego, most religions teach in some way that all of us must die before we die, and then we will not be afraid of dying. Suffering of some sort seems to be the only thing strong enough to destabilize our arrogance and our ignorance. I would define suffering very simply as whenever you are not in control."[98]

Feeling very out of control, I was finally released from the hospital. But without a nurse to support me in the care of my wounds and bodily functions, I was at a loss. That first night, at two in the morning, I went into the bathroom and desperately tried to reattach tubes and bags that were supposed to temporarily replace vital body parts. I was a mess. My body no longer functioned as it should, and modern medicine's solution was a pathetic shadow of how God had created me to be. My mind could not face the horror of such a future.

I threw the equipment across the room and collapsed on the floor, covered in my own bodily fluids, and began to weep. I had no words, only tears and self-pity.

Weeping and crying are different. Weeping requires your everything—your whole body. And when you're done, you feel empty, like you have nothing left inside.

And so I gave up and wept, because it was the only thing I could do.

The Hope of Water

Early the next morning, I awoke and cleaned myself up. Unfortunately, I hadn't been taken home to heaven during the night. As the dawn light streamed through the bathroom window, I sheepishly thought that I might be able to continue, at least one day at a time.

Over the coming days, God gave me an image of a jar of Mekong River water. I kept coming back to this image whenever I felt the anxiety pressing in again. The Mekong River is a broad brown sewer that runs through Cambodia and Vietnam; so at first the water in the jar looked murky and muddy. But when I placed the jar on a table, the silt in the water gradually sank to the bottom of the jar. As soon as I picked it up, everything churned up again, but the longer I left it in stillness, the clearer the water became.

In the same way, I sensed God calling me to rest in him and his peace. I heard his gentle whisper, *Be still and know that I am God.* In silence and solitude with God, I knew that my heart, mind, and soul would settle and clear. As writer and activist Phileena Heuertz has said, "Through activism we confront the toxicity in our world, through contemplation we confront the toxicity in ourselves."[99]

For years, I had pursued the heart of God through activism. The subversive Jesus I had come to know and love had placed a youthful passion in my heart for justice and the poor. But I had come close to burning myself out by pursuing his upside-down kingdom with my own strength.

Now God was subverting my drivenness and destabilizing my arrogance by calling me back to the things that would give me the power to continue for the long haul. In this complex dance between contemplation and action, I had been out of step too many times to mention, each foot tripping over the other. But it was a dance that I needed to stumble my way through.

Mother Teresa, who probably knew better than most what it meant to be a contemplative activist, said, "We need to find God, and he cannot be found in noise and restlessness. God is the friend of silence. See how nature—trees, flowers, grass—grows in silence; see the stars, the moon and the sun, how they move in silence . . . We need silence to be able to touch souls."[100]

This is not about external silence, which Mother Teresa would not have found in Calcutta, but rather an internal slowing down in order to become aware of God's presence.

Evenings at our home in the Downtown Eastside can feel overwhelming and out of control. Some of the homeless smell of the streets and unwashed socks. Many who are consumed by their addictions or mental illness have lost interest in personal hygiene. Some do not know what it means to talk quietly, including my own children—and Nay says they get it from me.

But regardless of what might have happened during our often chaotic house during the evening—whether a spontaneous jam session on the guitars, or the painful detoxing of someone withdrawing from crack—at nine o'clock, everyone knows it is our community's time to gather for listening prayer.

Drawing on the rich prayer tradition of St. Ignatius, we seek silence in the cloister within our hearts. We have learned from Ignatius that we don't have to retreat to a monastery to find space for prayer, but can be in silence together and become aware of God's presence amid our chaotic inner city neighborhood. And in that place of inner silence, we invite God to shine light on our day.

Where Faith Begins

During my dark days of struggle, I was acutely aware of my own privilege. I had access to free and expert healthcare, whereas colon cancer would likely mean death for our friends in Cambodian slums. And Nay and I had enough income to carry us through my recovery, thanks to our connections with churches and individuals who financially supported us. Our friends in the slum would have lost income the day they stopped working.

But as Nay and I considered the possibility that our children might be left without a father, our pain connected us even more deeply with the heartache of fatherless children around the globe. We realized at a very personal level that when we align ourselves with the poor and seek to be in solidarity with those Jesus called us to embrace, there will be a cost.

This was also true for Moses, who left the comfort of his Egyptian palace to align himself with a motley crowd of oppressed slaves. Though God offered Moses an exit plan, a chance to start again, he chose to stay with his people.[101] As a result of that choice, he spent the rest of his lifetime wandering in the desert, never entering the Promised Land.

And it was true for the prophet Elijah, who spoke out against King Ahab, a brutally exploitative ruler, for his unjust treatment of poor Naboth. Ahab killed Naboth so he could have his prime piece of real estate, and Elijah was forced to flee into exile.[102]

In the same way, Jeremiah, "the Weeping Prophet," spoke the truth to power and called the Hebrew nation to remember the poor. As a result, he was attacked by his own brothers, beaten and put into stocks, imprisoned by the king, threatened with death, and thrown into a cistern. No wonder the poor guy was always weeping!

Ezekiel, a contemporary of Jeremiah, proclaimed God's judgment against his people for practicing extortion and committing robbery, for oppressing the poor, and for mistreating the foreigner and denying them justice.[103] His wife died suddenly, and he was exiled along with those whom he was defending.

Following in the tradition of these ancient prophets, Jesus preached a gospel of repentance and good news for the poor. In his lowly birth, he aligned himself with the poor. And during his lifetime, he hung out with prostitutes and sinners, touched unclean lepers, and drank with outcasts, provoking the religious powers and wealthy elite to scorn and hate him. His friendships ultimately led to his execution as a common criminal.

Moses' commitment to the slaves took him to the wilderness. Elijah ended up in the desert, Jeremiah in prison. Ezekiel was deported. And Jesus finished his life on a cross.[104]

We say we want to be the hands and feet of Jesus in this broken world, but we forget that Jesus' hands and feet were pierced by nails.

As we share in the pain and suffering of the poor, we are invited to help close the gap between us and them, just as Jesus did. Standing with him in this gap is right where he wants us to be.

So we are left with this poignant question: Can you drink the cup of his suffering? Will you be a follower or merely an admirer?

CHAPTER 11

SUBVERSIVE
VOCATION

Normality is a paved road: it's comfortable to walk, but no flowers grow on it.

—VAN GOGH

Despite the pain, God was at work in the Downtown Eastside, and Nay and I came to see that the suffering we had experienced was not meaningless.

First, God brought punk rock Chuck into our home. From the red Mohawk on his head to the black leather boots on his feet, Chuck's body was covered in tattoos. His demons had chased him to the street and hounded him right to our door, where he came seeking Jesus and freedom from his addiction.

For two weeks that spring, Chuck lived with us while he struggled to get clean and waited for an opening in a drug rehabilitation program. He enjoyed the rhythms of prayer and food, the sense of community and laughter, the noisy joy of the kids.

When Chuck got into rehab, he was already professing a faith in Jesus, and the Twelve Step Program helped him flesh that out. By recognizing that he was unable to help himself and was in need of a higher power, Chuck turned everything over to God. He made a confession to everyone he had wounded and sought forgiveness from God and others. As Chuck grew in his faith, he began to provide leadership to others facing similar struggles within the program, and he held down a steady job.

Months later, Chuck stopped by the house to share a dream he'd had. "I want to help guys get off the streets by doing pre-hab in my own home like you guys," he told me. "A couple of us have gotten clean, and we're gonna do it together. We know what guys are going through. We know what it takes to help."

Deeply encouraged by his desire to serve others, I exclaimed, "That's awesome, bro!"

"It'll take some juggling because we all have construction jobs," he admitted. "But between us we think we can handle it."

As Chuck left our house, I thought of the story in Ezekiel 37, which had become a life theme for me. In this passage, God takes the prophet Ezekiel to a valley filled with dry bones. Ezekiel's valley of death and destruction reminded me of some parts of the Downtown Eastside, or slums where Nay and I had lived. Whenever people walked through these places, they often saw nothing but lifelessness, devastation, poverty, and oppression. And in the Downtown Eastside, many of the people's bodies have been emaciated by years of drug addiction, so they look like skin and bones.

When God asks Ezekiel if there is any life in this place of dry bones, Ezekiel answers in utter hopelessness, "God knows!"

At this point in the story, Ezekiel has already suffered

his own dry-bones experience. He lost his wife at a young age and has probably already grappled with the question of whether there can be life in the midst of death.[103]

Perhaps Ezekiel's words reflect the wider church's hopelessness about whether places of poverty and oppression can ever be transformed. "Only God knows!" we might think, as we go through the motions of our faith, engaging in charity once or twice a year, just to check the box.

But what if God's plans involve something more miraculous? What if God wants to raise up the dead and discarded, the broken and weak, the poor and oppressed ones we have already written off? What if God is working through former drug addicts like Chuck in Vancouver or orphans like Tom in Cambodia?

God commands Ezekiel to call the Spirit from the east and the west, the north and the south to breathe life into the dry bones scattered throughout that desolate valley.

Obediently, Ezekiel does what the Lord commands.

Immediately, the bones begin to rustle and stir. Flesh begins to appear. Slowly, the bones rise up and take on human form. Out of this place of death and destruction, God works a miracle, raising up a mighty army from among the dead and discarded.

As Lord over life and Lord over death, God can take our pain and our brokenness and transform it into something beautiful.

A Wasted Life Turned Around

When I first met Kevin, he had been mired in addiction—crack cocaine, alcohol, heroin—for most of his adult life.

Somehow, he stayed semifunctional for years, working hard as a plumbing foreman, counting the hours till his next hit, ignoring the hangovers when they crashed into him.

But one morning, at the age of forty-five, he woke up in a dingy, cockroach-infested hotel room in the Downtown Eastside. A bloody needle hung from his arm, and his body was racked with pain. Demons seemed to mock him from each corner of the room. If there was a hell, he figured this was it—and so he checked himself into rehab.

The guys at rehab took Kevin to church, though he was dubious about the religious scene and hadn't set foot in a church since he was a young boy.

I happened to be speaking about missions at the church where Kevin's friends brought him that Sunday, along with several others. Kevin sat in the back pew as I shared about the slums in Cambodia and the need for our love to extend to our brothers and sisters in other countries. As one speaker after another spoke of God's heart for the world and the poor, Kevin recalled a dream he had had three years earlier. He'd dreamed he was digging ditches and bringing water to a village. God whispered to Kevin, *This is the village. You should be digging ditches in Cambodia. That's what I made you for.*

Unable to hold back his tears, Kevin struggled to believe that God had spoken to him—a drug addict, an alcoholic, a "nobody" who had walked away from religion—and chosen him for a mission.

A couple of weeks later, Kevin tracked me down at my house. We shot some pool, and then he turned to me and said, "Craig, I think God is calling me to be a missionary to the slums in Cambodia. When can I go?"

I almost snorted my drink through my nose as I thought,

Two weeks ago you were hunched over a crack pipe. Now you're asking me when you can leave for Cambodia as a missionary? You've got to be kidding!

Struggling to regain my composure, I countered, "Well, there is quite a bit of preparation before you can go off and do something like that. Books to read, that kind of stuff."

"Help me, then," Kevin said earnestly. "I want to learn. I want to know more about Jesus and his heart for the poor. I want to know everything!"

From that day on, Kevin was a fixture in our home, arriving at seven thirty for our morning prayers and not leaving until after our nine o'clock evening prayers. In the hours between prayers, he ministered to whoever stopped by.

If Jeremiah was the Weeping Prophet, Kevin was the Weeping Preacher. He passionately shared his story, tearing up every time anyone would listen, especially those struggling with addiction.

Eventually, we invited him to move in, and he became an integral part of our community for the next couple of years.

Finally, the day came when we prayed and commissioned Kevin, and sent him to live in Cambodia.

Though it's been a tough road at times, filled with challenges and hardships, today Kevin lives with his Cambodian wife, Leakhana, and the people who were evicted from a city slum in a relocation site thirty minutes outside Phnom Penh. There, in that impoverished village, they have built dozens of houses for those made homeless by the eviction, along with a school and a beautiful community development ministry.[104] And yes, Kevin has dug a ditch or two.

God is transforming death into life—raising a miraculous army from among a heap of dry bones.

Finding Your Own Calcutta

Kevin found his calling in Cambodia. But not everyone is called to the slums.

When a friend asked me whether his lack of interest in the poor made him a bad Christian, I asked him what he was passionate about. "I am a nurse. I am passionate about helping sick people," he said.

"Then you have found your vocation. Serve Jesus with all your heart in the hospital."

Another friend asked if the call she felt to minister to university students from affluent backgrounds was valid.

"Of course. Who will love them if you don't? Teach them to establish the subversive upside-down kingdom of Jesus. Those young people need to know God's heart for the poor as much as anyone because they will be the nation's leaders."

The Bible tells us that Abraham practiced hospitality and God was with him. We also hear that Elijah loved to pray and God was with him. And we read about how David ruled a kingdom and God was with him too.

If you are seeking the work God has made you to do, search for the deepest inclination of your heart and follow it to where it meets the suffering of the world.[105]

Or in the words of Mother Teresa, "Find your own Calcutta." If you can't feed a hundred people, then feed the one God places in front of you. You must resist the temptation to do nothing because you can do only a little or because you can't be like someone else who seems more radical. It takes many tiny candles to overcome the darkness.

There is nothing prescriptive about the stories I have shared in this book. The stories are merely demonstrations of how God has worked in my life and the lives of those around me. How God led us to live and minister in Cambodia looks completely different from how God led us to live and minister in Vancouver. If we were in Tokyo or London, Seattle or Brisbane, it would look very different again.

Your work is to discern how God has uniquely wired you to follow Jesus, our subversive Savior, and build his upside-down kingdom in the ruins of a crumbling empire—and to keep following him all the way to the cross. As we journeyed together through this season of grieving, suffering, and joyful celebrating, Nay and I sensed that God was beckoning us toward a new Calcutta.

With Kevin's relocation to Cambodia and my fortieth birthday around the corner, I began to review my priorities. My brush with death had pushed me to consider how I would spend my last five years on this planet, if that was all I had left. I still wasn't sure how long I might have, since the cancer could return at any time.

As I held this question before God, I immediately thought of my own children, who might have been left without a father. And then I thought of the fatherless children I knew from the slums of Cambodia, who didn't have anyone to walk alongside them.

And without a moment's hesitation, I knew that if I were given only five more years, I would pour them out for the vulnerable children in the developing world. Yet for the first time in my life, as my mind filled with uncertainties and an awareness of my own weakness, I wondered if I had what it would take to embark on something new.

"Lord, I can barely get on a plane."

I will give you strength.

"Lord, what about the people here in Vancouver? The friends who need us?"

You're not indispensable. I have the body of Christ.

"What about Nay? She loves it here."

For this question, God led me to the story of Mary. She heard from the angel Gabriel about the things God was about to do. Then I noticed a gap I had never seen before.

There must have been a gap—perhaps even a few months—between when Gabriel spoke to Mary, before she had even conceived, and when he sent an angel to speak to Joseph in a dream, after Mary was already pregnant.[106]

I trusted that Nay would hear from God too, according to his timing.

As I continued to recover from cancer, we realized that we would need to travel back to New Zealand to access the free healthcare and support of family there. So we prepared to leave our community in the Downtown Eastside in the capable hands of those who had journeyed alongside us.

Three and a half years after my first claustrophobic episode in London's Tube, I boarded a plane at Vancouver Airport. With fear and trembling, I settled in for the long flight to our home in New Zealand—where, in time, I trusted that our family would begin winding our way toward our new Calcutta.

— EPILOGUE —

OUR NEW
CALCUTTA

Over the next several months, as our plans unfolded, I didn't know if we would return to live in North America or if we would be based somewhere else. One day, as Nay and I sat quietly on the side of one of the beautiful mountain ranges in New Zealand's North Island, she turned to me and said, "I think we should move back to Cambodia."

I nodded my head, trying not to react immediately. Being in Cambodia would make sense. We wanted the Alongsiders movement to grow out of the developing world, and Cambodia was where it all had begun. And logically, our startup and operations costs would be much cheaper there. But I wanted to confirm that God was in it and that it made sense for our family.

"Are you sure?" I asked, turning to face Nay. "You love Vancouver."

"Yes. But I think God is calling us to Cambodia for this next season."

I broke into a big smile and drew Nay close to me. In his time, God had been stirring us both toward the same thing.

After convincing the doctors, we would be free to begin making preparations for our move. Several months later, as I met with my doctor to review the results of a surgical biopsy of my lymph nodes, he told me, "Mr. Greenfield, it appears unlikely that the cancer has spread." I was cancer-free, for now.

As I left the doctor's office, I gave thanks and wondered how God would use the bonus years he had given me. Subversively, I hoped.

After we relocated back to Cambodia, we rented a new home in a tiny slum community on the outskirts of Phnom Penh, just half a mile from where we had been evicted a decade previously. This is the vibrant community where we continue to live today, as this book is being written.

From our years in the Downtown Eastside, we knew how important it was to reach children before they become hardened by dysfunction and addiction. We had seen God work through the Alongsiders movement in Cambodia as it transformed the lives of hundreds of children and spread into various provinces. Now we hoped to see it working in other countries and continents.

Inspired by the vision of Ezekiel 37, we dreamed about how the Alongsiders movement might raise up young Christians—the poorest of the poor themselves—throughout the developing world. We knew they were the ones who would reach the next generation of vulnerable children.

As we held on to the image of the valley of dry bones in Ezekiel, we imagined an army of tens of thousands of youth, reaching out to abandoned, neglected, and orphaned children in their own communities, leading the way in transforming their own slums and rural villages around the world.

One day, my young Cambodian friend Tom pulled me aside for a word. Tom had been one of the first little brothers and was now leading a group of eighteen Alongsiders as a youth pastor in his slum community.

"I've got some good news to share." He smiled broadly. "I've fallen in love . . . and gotten engaged to one of the other Alongsiders from my village."

Before I could ask, Tom grinned. "Yes, of course you know her—it's Srey Ta!"

Srey Ta was one of the first little sisters, a girl I had known since she tragically lost her father at eleven years of age. She had grown into an amazing young woman who taught pre-schoolers at the local church. Srey Ta loved God and loved children.

Tom's forehead creased, and he looked serious for a moment. "I have a problem, though. I d-don't have any parents to be with me at the wedding," he stuttered nervously. "Do you think . . . I mean . . . would you and Aunty Nay be willing to be my father and mother for this special occasion?" Tom looked at the ground sheepishly.

I knew that Cambodian weddings are highly ceremonial and require full family participation. The parents of the bride and groom take on an honored role in the celebration. So I reached out and placed a hand on Tom's shoulder, my eyes blinking back tears of gratitude to God. "Nothing would be a greater honor for us, Tom. We would love to stand with you on that important day."

This audacious dream to see the poor rising up and becoming leaders, becoming godly men and women, was bearing fruit into the second generation. I sensed God confirming that I was to stand alongside them. A dream like this, to reach the world's most vulnerable children, was worth pouring out our lives for, even if we could reach only one young man like Tom and one young woman like Srey Ta. The sacrifice had been well worth it.

Not knowing whether we would sink or swim, I was amazed when just twelve months after we arrived back in Asia, we were able to sign an agreement with a network of three thousand Dalit (formerly "untouchable") churches across India to begin equipping the youth for an Alongsiders network. Together, we began working toward the dream of reaching millions of the Dalit-caste children in India. Around the same time, we formed a partnership with a similar church network in Indonesia to equip their Christian youth to become Alongsiders and reach out to Muslim children. As I write these words, seeds of a discipleship movement among the poor are germinating in several more countries across Asia, Africa, and the Middle East. Wherever I go, people are excited about equipping young Christians in the non-Western world to care for their neighbors and to walk alongside vulnerable children. People love the idea of the poor being raised up to help the poor, and they are inspired as they imagine the fast-growing developing world church playing a central role. As a result, the developing church will be less dependent on Western finances and will have the potential to make a broad and deep impact on local communities.

As God faithfully continues to establish his subversive, upside-down kingdom among the poorest of the poor, I am grateful for the extra time I have been given to be his hands and feet in a suffering world. I can speak subversive words with passion and conviction because I see firsthand how he is turning this broken world upside down. God is good. He is truly good.

AUTHOR'S NOTE

For a free *Subversive Jesus* small group study guide and *Subversive Jesus* audio book:

www.craiggreenfield.com

www.facebook.com/CraigWGreenfield

craig@alongsiders.org

To learn more about Alongsiders International:

www.alongsiders.org

www.facebook.com/Alongsiders

info@alongsiders.org

ACKNOWLEDGMENTS

Without the example of my parents, who lived lives of radical hospitality before we gave it an edgy name, I would not be who I am today. Thank you, Mum and Dad. From generation to generation. To my children, Jayden and Micah: I know this book and the life we have lived have cost you some time with Daddy that was rightfully yours. Thank you for sharing me with others. To Nay, my wise and steady partner in love and mission for over eighteen years and counting: I owe you everything.

For my friends and coworkers in Servants to Asia's Urban Poor and Alongsiders International: I learned the ways of Jesus because of your sacrificial example in serving. To Helen Sidebotham, my humble, faithful, tenacious friend: your memory lives on. To Ruth, Jason and Laura, Tom and Ash, Kevin, Justin, John Baird, Carlos, Elisabeth, and so many others who walked alongside us in the DTES: you guys are the best companions I could have asked for.

Thanks to Dave Diewert, Dave Andrews, Charles Ringma, and Kristin Jack, who inspired the theological reflections in this tome more than you may realize. Thanks and kudos to my editor, Karen Hollenbeck Wuest, who massaged this story into a readable form and challenged me when you felt sure I was going astray. I needed that. Thanks to my agent, Jenni Burke, who fought for this. Thanks to Carolyn at Zondervan, who believed.

NOTES

1. Shane Claiborne, *The Irresistible Revolution: Living as an Ordinary Radical* (Grand Rapids: Zondervan, 2006), 32.
2. My memory, like everyone else's, is fallible, and some of my recollections are probably inaccurate. Most of these stories and conversations have been recreated to reflect the heart of what was spoken rather than the actual words, which have been lost to time. I've also changed a few names to protect the privacy of friends.
3. Luke 4:18.
4. I am grateful to Kristin Jack for pointing out this example of how a lack of truly holistic discipleship can turn out so badly. The paragraphs about Rwanda are adapted from his writing.
5. *www.servantsasia.org.*
6. Frank Viola, "An Interview with Brian Zahnd," *Frank Viola: The Deeper Journey*, May 8, 2015, *http://www .patheos.com/blogs/frankviola/brianzahnd/.*
7. Donald Kraybill, *The Upside-Down Kingdom* (Scottdale, PA: Herald Press, 1978), is credited with coining the term upside-down kingdom.
8. Dietrich Bonhoeffer, *The Mystery of the Holy Night*, ed. Manfred Weber (New York: Crossroad, 1996), 6 (trans. by Peter Heinegg from Bonhoeffer, *Werke*, volume 9).
9. Luke 4:28–29.
10. Oscar Romero, *The Violence of Love* (Maryknoll, NY: Orbis, 2004), 44.

11. Mark 11:15–19; Matt. 21:12–17; Luke 19:45–48; John 2:13–16.

12. Matt. 8:20.

13. Luke 14:12–14, emphasis added.

14. Matt. 25:43.

15. Stanley Hauerwas, *The Stanley Hauerwas Reader*, ed. John Berkman and Michael Cartwright (Durham, NC: Duke University Press, 2001), 502. This quotation and subsequent thoughts on marriage were inspired by Daniel Oudshoorn, "On Loving My Wife," *On Journeying with Those in Exile* (blog), September 8, 2008, *http://poserorprophet.wordpress.com/2008/09/08/on-loving-my-wife/*.

16. Gustavo Gutiérrez, *We Drink from Our Own Wells: The Spiritual Journey of a People* (Maryknoll, NY: Orbis, 2003), 7.

17. Luke 2:1.

18. Luke 3:12–14.

19. This section on the contrast between empire and the kingdom of God is inspired by a similar piece by Tom Sine: *The New Conspirators: Creating the Future One Mustard Seed at a Time* (Downers Grove, IL: InterVarsity, 2008), 120.

20. Luke 8:3.

21. Our relationship with local churches was also inspired by St. Francis, who submitted to the Catholic Church but built a radical community on the edge of the institution. The Catholic Church was blessed by the life and new energy stirred up by the Franciscans, and in turn Francis's fledgling community was resourced and supported by the Church. Likewise, we felt we should attend and submit to local Christian leadership, while at the same time maintaining our distinct calling and charism. So, after some time of visiting local churches and praying, each

community member would bring their choice of church to the wider community, and we would prayerfully commission them to join that congregation.

22. Janet Poppendieck, *Sweet Charity? Emergency Food and the End of Entitlement* (New York: Penguin, 1998), 251.

23. Quoted in Christine D. Pohl, *Making Room: Hospitality as a Christian Tradition* (Grand Rapids: Eerdmans, 1999), 132.

24. Luke 4:18.

25. Num. 14:3.

26. Matt. 18:3.

27. In those days, I was leading Servants to Asia's Urban Poor, a beautiful and radical incarnational mission agency training up and sending missionaries to live in Asian slums. Check them out if you are interested in slum ministry: *www.servantsasia.org.*

28. Dr. Babatunde Osotimehin, Executive Director of UNFPA, the United Nations Population Fund, writing in *The Atlantic, http://www.theatlantic.com/international/ archive/2012/11/young-people-have-the-power-to- change-the-world/265200/.* The Western world faces declining populations as our population bulge edges its way toward retirement, but the face of the developing world is unwrinkled, shining with hope and optimism. In Cambodia, more than two-thirds of the population is under thirty. This youth bulge presents major challenges in a country still rebuilding after a devastating war that few knew firsthand. There are not enough jobs, especially for young men like Tom. The burgeoning garment industry absorbs young girls from the countryside, and they toil long hours over sewing machines in sweatshops, making Gap jeans and Old Navy T-shirts for a couple of dollars a day, if they are lucky. But young men often find themselves with little to contribute.

29. Mark 10:17–22.

30. Mark 10:26, 29–30.
31. Luke 4:18.
32. Matt. 26:52.
33. Matt. 5:44.
34. Matt. 21:31.
35. Aleksandr Solzhenitsyn, *The Gulag Archipelago* (New York: Harper Perennial, 2007), 312.
36. Thomas Merton, *New Seeds of Contemplation* (New York: New Directions, 2007), 177.
37. Matt. 16:21.
38. Matt. 16:22–23.
39. Matt. 16:24–26.
40. The phrase "holy mischief" is commonly attributed to Shane Claiborne. For example, Shane Claiborne, "A Season for Mischief and Conspiracy: A New Take on Christmas Charity," *Huffington Post*, December 5, 2010, *http://www .huffingtonpost.com/shane-claiborne/a-season-for-holy-mischie_b_790149.html*.
41. Dave Andrews, "The Subversive Spirituality of Christi-Anarchy," *DaveAndrews.com.au, http://www .daveandrews.com.au/articles/The%20Subversive%20 Spirituality%20Of%20Christi-Anarchy.pdf*.
42. Matt. 5:9.
43. Quoted in Carl C. Hodge and Cathal J. Nolan, eds., *U.S. Presidents and Foreign Policy* (Santa Barbara, CA: ABC Clio, 2007), 279.
44. Martin Luther King Jr., "Beyond Vietnam: A Time to Break Silence," Martin Luther King Jr. and the Global Freedom Struggle, *http://kingencyclopedia.stanford.edu/ encyclopedia/documentsentry/doc_beyond_vietnam*.
45. Glen H. Stassen and David P. Gushee, *Kingdom Ethics: Following Jesus in Contemporary Context* (Downers Grove, IL: InterVarsity, 2003).
46. John 9:2.

47. Quoted in Robert H. Bremner, *American Philanthropy* (Chicago: University of Chicago Press, 1988), 42.

48. Poppendieck, *Sweet Charity?* 5.

49. Quoted in Howard Zinn and Anthony Arnove, *Voices of a People's History of the United States* (New York: Seven Stories Press, 2004), 426.

50. Ninety-six percent of charitable foundation board members in the United States are white, and 77 percent are men. INCITE! Women of Color against Violence, ed., *The Revolution Will Not Be Funded: Beyond the Non-Profit Industrial Complex* (Boston: South End Press, 2009).

51. Matt. 6:1.

52. For this reason, Greenpeace has been denied charitable status by many governments. Blake Bromley, "The CRA Should Learn That Charities Can Have Controversial Views," *Huffington Post*, August 7, 2014, *http://www .huffingtonpost.ca/blake-bromley/greenpeace-new-zealand_b_5658588.html*.

53. Ex. 9:1.

54. Mark 1:14–15, emphasis added.

55. Luke 17:33.

56. Luke 18:22; Mark 10:21; Matt. 19:21.

57. Luke 19:8.

58. Luke 19:9.

59. Whenever we discuss the renunciation of possessions, there is the danger that it can become legalistic. "There's a guru in India who says, 'Every time a prostitute comes to me, she's talking about nothing but God. She says, "I'm sick of this life that I'm living. I want God." But every time a priest comes to me he's talking about nothing but sex.' When you renounce something, you become fixated with it. When you fight against something, you somehow become more tied to it. As long as you're fighting it, you are giving it power" (Anthony de Mello, SJ). This is the

problem with trying to live simply. The key is not to pursue sacrifice, nor to renounce things. The key is to seek to understand their place, examine the hold they have over you, and then focus on pursuing something even better—radical and beautiful generosity.

60. Luke 19:9–10.
61. Luke 16:19–31.
62. Luke 16:31.
63. Luke 19:8.
64. Ricky passed away before the publication of this book.
65. If you are interested in a slum immersion learning experience, contact Servants to learn more about their internship program (www.servantsasia.org).
66. This is not to say there is no place in the world for one-way relationships. We all need services, and we don't necessarily want to get to know our bank teller or hang out with our mortgage broker on weekends. But if you think carefully about the relationships that have been the most transformative in your life, they are all mutual relationships that go much deeper than the one-way, transactional type.
67. John 13:1–17.
68. Isa. 20:2; Mic. 1:8.
69. Jeremiah 13.
70. Mark 6:14–29.
71. Luke 9:5.
72. Amos 8:4.
73. Isa. 1:17.
74. Jer. 22:13.
75. Ezek. 16:49.
76. Mic. 6:8.
77. Zech. 7:9–10.
78. 1 Kings 18:4.
79. Luke 11:42.

80. Howard Zinn, *The Howard Zinn Reader: Writings on Disobedience and Democracy* (New York: Seven Stories, 2009), 420.

81. Matt. 10:19–20.

82. Mark 3:2–6.

83. Father John Dear, "Civil Disobedience and Discipleship to Jesus," *FatherJohnDear.org*, http://www.fatherjohndear .org/articles/civil-disobedience-jesus.html.

84. Juliet Eilperin, "Obama Promised to Curb the Influence of Lobbyists. Has He Succeeded?" *Washington Post*, March 22, 2015, http://www.washingtonpost.com/ politics/obama-promised-to-curb-the-influence- of-lobbyists-has-he-succeeded/2015/03/22/ e9ec766e-ab03-11e4-abe8-e1ef60ca26de_story.html.

85. Ronald J. Sider, *Rich Christians in an Age of Hunger*, 2nd. ed. (Downers Grove, IL: InterVarsity, 1984), 192.

86. Luke 13:10–17.

87. Luke 14:1–6.

88. John 5:1–18.

89. Matt. 15:1–9.

90. Matt. 12:1–8.

91. Matt. 21:12–17.

92. Acts 4:19–20.

93. 1 Peter 2:13–15.

94. Rom. 13:1–2.

95. Eph. 6:1, 5.

96. Matt. 5:39.

97. Anthony de Mello, *Awareness* (New York: Image Books, 1990), 147.

98. Richard Rohr, *Yes, and . . .: Daily Meditations* (Cincinnati: Franciscan Media, 2013), 273.

99. Scott A. Bessenecker, ed., *Living Mission: The Vision and Voices of New Friars* (Downers Grove, IL: InterVarsity Press, 2010), 117.

100. S. Conroy, *Mother Theresa's Lessons of Love and Secrets of Sanctity* (Huntington, IN: Our Sunday Visitor Publishing Division, 2003), 120.
101. Ex. 32:9–14.
102. 1 Kings 21.
103. Ezek. 22:29.
104. I am grateful for these thoughts from Mick Duncan in an unpublished work, *Discipleship and Suffering*, edited by Dorothy Harris.
105. Ezek. 24:18.
106. To learn more about Kevin and Leakhana's ministry, visit *www.manna4lifecambodia.org*.
107. Anthony de Mello, *One Minute Wisdom* (New York: Doubleday, 1985), 15.
108. Matt. 1:20.